REVISE AQA GCSE (9–1)
History
AMERICA, 1840–1895: EXPANSION AND CONSOLIDATION

REVISION
GUIDE AND WORKBOOK

Series Consultant: Harry Smith

Authors: Sally Clifford and Julia Robertson

Also available to support your revision:

Revise GCSE Study Skills Guide   9781447967071

The **Revise GCSE Study Skills Guide** is full of tried-and-trusted hints and tips for how to learn more effectively. It gives you techniques to help you achieve your best – throughout your GCSE studies and beyond!

Revise GCSE Revision Planner   9781447967828

The **Revise GCSE Revision Planner** helps you to plan and organise your time, step-by-step, throughout your GCSE revision. Use this book and wall chart to mastermind your revision.

For the full range of Pearson revision titles across KS2, KS3, GCSE, Functional Skills, AS/A Level and BTEC visit:
www.pearsonschools.co.uk/revise

Contents

. . . .

A small bit of small print

AQA publishes Sample Assessment Material and the Specification on its website. This is the official content and this book should be used in conjunction with it.

The questions and revision tasks in this book have been written to help you revise the skills you may need for your assessment. Remember: the real assessment may not look like this.

The Great American Desert

In 1840, white settlers thought that the Great Plains were an inhospitable desert. North America's many natural frontiers made it hard to cross the continent to settle.

> **Inhospitable** means harsh and difficult to live in. A **frontier** is a border between two areas.

The landscape of North America, 1840

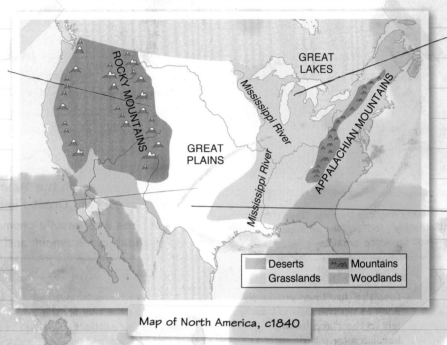

The American West: the two-thirds of North America to the west of the Mississippi River

Snow-belts: areas of very heavy snowfall in winter

ROCKY MOUNTAINS

GREAT LAKES

Mississippi River

APPALACHIAN MOUNTAINS

GREAT PLAINS

Mississippi River

An enormous, natural grassland stretching from north to south between the Mississippi River in the east and the Rocky Mountains in the west

Before the name Great Plains was given, the area was known as 'The Great American Desert'

Deserts   Mountains
Grasslands   Woodlands

Map of North America, c1840

Attitudes to the Great American Desert

> This region is almost wholly unfit for cultivation and farmers cannot hope to live on this land. Occasionally there are large areas of fertile land but the shortage of wood and water will mean settling the country is impossible ...
>
> *American explorer, Major Stephen H Long (1784–1864)*

In 1819, Major Long was sent to explore the lands west of the Mississippi River. Afterwards, he published a report and map that led to the Great Plains being called 'The Great American Desert'.

You will need to know the main natural features which led to the attitude that the American West could not be lived in.

Inhospitable conditions

Until the 1840s, the American government and people living east of the Appalachian Mountains believed that the Great Plains were not inhabitable (fit to live in) due to:

- a lack of trees, meaning that it was hard to find wood to build with
- dry conditions, with very little water
- scorching hot summer winds
- its flat, featureless landscape
- bitterly cold winter conditions
- from November to March, harsh winds called 'Blue-Northers' causing sudden drops in temperature and heavy rain
- the presence of dangerous wolves
- the presence of locusts, which would ruin crops.

Now try this

Write a short paragraph to explain why people thought the Great American Desert was uninhabitable. Include at least **three** natural features of the land in your answer.

'Manifest Destiny'

'Manifest Destiny' was the idea that it was the God-given right of white Americans to expand westwards across North America. It was a concept that would have huge importance in the settlement of the West and the attitudes of white settlers to the Plains Indians.

The painting *American Progress* by John Gast (1872) shows 'Manifest Destiny', looking like an angel, leading the way west for white settlers.

The idea of 'Manifest Destiny'

☑ White Americans saw themselves as a superior race. They believed they had the right to populate all of North America from the east coast to the west coast.

☑ It was their mission (God's will) to spread westwards across North America.

☑ By populating all of North America they would spread democracy and Protestantism.

☑ The white settlers were compelled by God to establish the 'American way of life' across the Great Plains.

☑ The idea was heavily promoted by the American government and newspapers.

Land that had been previously seen as worthless, and best left to the Plains Indians, became a target for settling.

The Plains Indians had to make way for the white settlers, causing conflict and unrest.

White Americans were comfortable with the idea of clearing the Plains Indians out of the way as it was 'God's will'.

The importance of 'Manifest Destiny'

Americans gained access to new resources, such as gold and silver, strengthening the American economy.

For more on 'push' and 'pull' factors, see page 5.

'Manifest Destiny' became a major 'pull' factor in **migration** from the East to the Great Plains.

The size of America increased.

The origin of 'Manifest Destiny'

The phrase 'Manifest Destiny' was first used by John L. O'Sullivan, the founder of the *United States Magazine* and the *Democratic Review*. He used the phrase in an article in 1845, in which he encouraged the expansion of North America all the way to California in the West.

'Manifest Destiny' continued to be a key factor in the settlement of the West all the way through to the 1860s and 1870s.

For more on the role of 'Manifest Destiny' in the settling of homesteaders in the West, see page 24.

Now try this

Write a short paragraph to explain how the painting above symbolises 'Manifest Destiny'.

The Mormons: persecution

The Mormons are a good example of why people moved west and the challenges early settlers faced. **Persecution** (treating others in a cruel way because of race, religion, politics, or some other difference) in the East meant the Mormons headed west.

Joseph Smith and the Mormons

In 1830, Joseph Smith founded the Church of Jesus Christ of Latter-day Saints, known as the **Mormons.** He believed that an angel had given him a book from God, and his persuasive manner meant that he quickly attracted followers. He was assassinated in 1844.

Why were the Mormons persecuted?

Religious and political reasons: The movement grew very quickly, which worried people.

Religious and political reasons: The Mormons moved in large numbers, causing tensions with existing communities.

Political and economic reasons: People were angry about the financial crash and wanted someone to blame.

Other reasons: **The Danites**, a Mormon militia group, were often violent towards non-Mormons.

Political and economic reasons: Americans worried that Smith was planning to overthrow the United States government and disrupt the economy.

Political and economic reasons: The Mormons encouraged freedom for slaves.

Religious reasons: People were against the practice of **polygamy.**

Religious reasons: The Mormons claimed to be Christians, but other Christians were offended by their new **religion.**

Other reasons: The Mormons were very private and did not mix with non-Mormons.

Mormon history, 1831–1848

In **1831**, after being arrested in New York and fearing further persecution, Smith and his wife left for **Kirtland, Ohio**, where they built a huge temple.

In **1833**, a mob destroyed the Mormons' printing office in **Independence, Missouri**.

In **1838**, Smith fled to **Missouri** after the bank that he set up in Kirtland went bankrupt during the financial crash.

In **October 1838**, after Mormons attacked a unit of state militia at the **Battle of Crooked River**, the governor issued an order expelling the Mormons from Missouri. A mob then massacred a group of Mormons at **Haun's Mill**. Smith was arrested and sentenced to death for **treason** but the executioner refused to kill him and Smith spent the next five months in prison.

By **early 1839**, the Mormons were forced out of Missouri. Brigham Young helped to relocate them to **Nauvoo, Illinois.**

In **April 1839**, Smith escaped from prison and travelled to Nauvoo.

By **1843**, rumours of controversial new practices introduced by Smith, such as **polygamy** (being married to more than one person at the same time), had spread and anti-Mormon feeling grew again.

In **1844**, Smith was arrested after ordering his followers to destroy a newspaper company. While in prison he was shot by a mob.

In **1846**, thousands of Mormons left Nauvoo led by Brigham Young and suffered difficult winter conditions on the march west.

In **1847**, an advance party reached the **Great Salt Lake**, outside the boundaries of the United States.

By **1848**, thousands of followers had left the winter camp in Iowa and reached the **Great Salt Lake**.

Now try this

List **two** religious reasons and **two** economic reasons why the Mormons were persecuted.

The Mormons: Great Salt Lake

In 1847–1848 the Mormons settled in the **Salt Lake Valley**, which was then part of Mexico. Brigham Young was a key figure in the organisation and was a vital part of the success of the Mormons' move to the valley, where they built Salt Lake City.

Brigham Young

Brigham Young became a Mormon in 1832 and rose to become the second leader of the Church. When Joseph Smith was murdered in 1844, Young took control of the Church. In 1846, he led the Mormons out of Illinois. He was president (official leader of the Church) from 1847 until his death and is widely believed to be the reason behind the success of the Mormons settling in the Salt Lake Valley.

The journey west: problems and solutions

Problem: The journey to the Salt Lake Valley was very dangerous and there were a lot of people to move.

Solution: Young organised a count of all the people and wagons they had to move (about 3000 families in 2500 wagons), so he was able to plan carefully.

Solution: The migrants were divided into small groups; each group had a leader.

Solution: To avoid arguments and make sure that people knew what to do if they were split up, Young gave everyone a specific job and insisted on strict discipline.

Problem: The Mormons did not know what to expect when they got to the Salt Lake Valley.

Solution: Young spoke to a number of guides, including Plains Indians, to find out as much as he could about the destination so they could prepare thoroughly.

Settling in the Salt Lake Valley: problems and solutions

Problem: Life in the Salt Lake Valley was very hard, the land was very dry and there were no trees for wood.

Solution: Irrigation systems (to supply water for crops) were quickly organised to divert water from the melting snow in the mountains.

Solution: Houses could not be made from wood, so they used mud bricks.

Solution: Young's strict leadership was crucial. His followers believed that he was sent by God and so they obeyed him.

Problem: The Mormons had to be able to produce everything they needed.

Solution: Young declared that the Church owned all the land and that everyone must work together for the good of the community. Settlements were organised carefully, with each one producing something different under the leadership of a Church elder (a leader with authority).

Solution: Settlements further away from the Lake had to send products back to Salt Lake City.

Problem: The area was part of Mexico when the Mormons arrived in 1848, but was soon occupied by the American government.

Solution: Young declared the settlement part of a separate state called Deseret.

Solution: To begin with it looked as if the Mormons and the American government would go to war. However, Young eventually came to a compromise with the government and the area became part of the new territory of Utah in 1850.

Now try this

Write a short paragraph to explain **one** problem the Mormons faced when they moved to the Great Salt Lake and how they overcame it.

Journey west: push and pull

There were many different reasons why people decided to make the long and dangerous journey west. Some of these factors pushed migrants away from the East, while others pulled them west, to places like California and Oregon.

Pull factors for moving west

For more on 'Manifest Destiny', see page 2. For more on the Oregon Trail, see page 6. For more on the California Gold Rush, turn to page 7.

Push factors for moving west

👍 Freedom and independence

👍 Free farming land

👍 Government promotion

👍 'Manifest Destiny'

👍 Positive stories from traders and fur-trappers

👍 Oregon Trail

👍 Gold

👎 Financial crisis of 1837

👎 Overpopulation

👎 Persecution

👎 Unemployment

Timeline

Moving west

1837 Financial crisis causes economic depression: people lose savings, wages are cut and unemployment increases. Wheat prices fall; many farmers face ruin.

1845 The phrase 'Manifest Destiny' is first used.

1847 Mormons reach Salt Lake Valley.

1849 200 000 people travel to California.

1874 Gold is discovered in the Black Hills (Dakota).

1836 The first migrants to travel the Oregon Trail by wagon reach their destination.

1841 Government funds John Frémont (explorer and mapmaker) to map the Oregon Trail and they publish a guide book.

1846 Governor of Illinois tells Mormons to leave the state.

1848 Gold is discovered in the Sierra Nevada.

1858–1859 Gold is discovered in the Rocky Mountains.

Although some of the events mentioned here took place before 1840, it is important that you know them so you can write about factors that made the early settlers decide to go west.

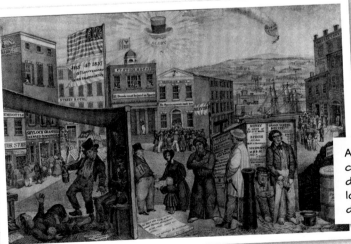

A cartoon from the *Times* newspaper commenting on hardship in New York City during the 1837 economic crisis. Many people lost their jobs, businesses and savings and decided that life would be better in the West.

Now try this

Explain **one** push and **one** pull factor, which led early settlers to move west.

Journey west: pioneer trails

The pioneer trails which led west were established to show migrant farmers the best way to get to the West. They were often dangerous – even when the trails were followed disaster could strike.

The journey west

There was a fear of attacks by Plains Indians but these were rare. Plains Indians were more likely to help travellers than attack them.

Migrants began the trail in April, in Independence, Missouri, when there would be enough grass on the Plains for their animals.

Crossing the Great Plains was made dangerous by: extreme temperatures, storms, disease, stampeding buffalo, and running out of supplies.

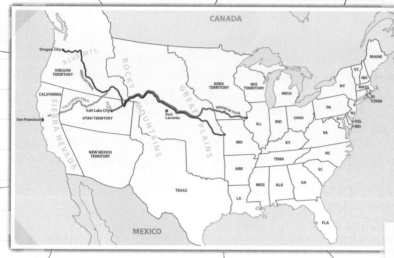

The biggest danger came from illness; cholera and dysentery, in particular, killed many.

Wagons were hauled across the mountain terrain using chains, ropes and pulleys. Injuries were common.

Migrants needed to take supplies for the entire journey.

Early migrants used explorers or Plains Indians as guides; later migrants relied on guidebooks.

Pioneer trails taken by migrant farmers going west

Most people used strong oxen to pull the loaded wagons, but oxen were also very slow. Timescales for the journey were tight and delays could lead to disaster.

The safest way to travel was in large groups of 20 or more wagons, known as wagon trains. These would often contain people with a mix of skills that would be useful along the way.

Each trail crossed two mountain ranges: the Rockies, and either the Blue Mountains or the Sierra Nevada. They were steep, and bad weather meant that people often froze to death.

Migrants going west

Donner Party, 1846

In May 1846, the Donner family set off for California as part of a train of almost 500 wagons. They suffered many hardships, and only 46 of the 87 members of the party survived to reach California because:
- Arguments divided the group over whether to take a largely untested route.
- The shortcut cost time, wagons and livestock as they tried to pass through difficult terrain.
- With supplies running out, arguments started, and one man was murdered.
- Snow and delays caused by the shortcut left them stranded alone through the winter.
- They had to eat animal skins, and eventually resorted to cannibalism in order to survive.

Sagar Party, 1844

In April 1844, Naomi and Henry Sagar set out along the Oregon Trail with their six children. Their daughter Catherine later wrote down what happened during the journey:
- Extreme rain and mud slowed their progress.
- Naomi Sagar gave birth to her seventh child during the journey and never fully recovered.
- Catherine Sagar broke her leg jumping off a wagon.
- Many of the travellers got sick with 'camp fever' (typhus), which killed both Henry and Naomi and left their children as orphans.

Gould Party, 1862

The Gould party consisted of Jane Gould, her husband Albert and their two sons. Jane kept a diary of her experiences, detailing the hardships they faced, including:
- the extreme cold, wind and rain of the Great Plains and Utah desert
- running out of supplies
- cattle stampedes
- attacks by Plains Indians
- crossing the harsh terrain of the Rocky Mountains and the Sierra Nevada.

Now try this

Imagine you are a survivor of the Donner Party. In a short paragraph, describe the challenges you faced on your journey west.

The miners

In 1848, gold was discovered in California, leading to a **gold rush** in 1849. Large numbers of migrants headed west with major consequences for both California and America as a whole.

The pull of gold

The biggest 'pull' factor for migrants heading to California was gold.

- It was first discovered in the Sierra Nevada in 1848.
- By April 1849 over 200 000 people had left the East and set off in the hope of finding gold and becoming rich.
- Life for a gold prospector was hard and not everyone was successful.
- Many spent their life savings travelling to the area and buying their equipment, but most did not find gold.

Prospectors (people who search for gold) came from all over the world and, by 1855, 300 000 had settled in California. At first it was mainly men who set up in temporary camps hoping to make a fortune and then return home. However, they were soon joined by female servants and prostitutes, and later by their families.

The California Gold Rush

CALIFORNIA

CALIFORNIA TRAIL

SIERRA NEVADA

Sutter's Fort

San Francisco

☐ Gold mining area
☐ Most gold found

Map showing important locations in the California Gold Rush

Those who set off along the Oregon Trail in 1849 were later known as the '49ers'.

The effects of the Gold Rush

Positive	Negative
👍 The Gold Rush helped the American economy to recover from its financial problems.	👎 Problems with Plains Indians due to increased use of the Oregon Trail.
👍 Farming in California grew into a strong industry and California's economy grew quickly as prospectors needed food, equipment and entertainment.	👎 Widespread lawlessness in mining camps, including murder of Californian Indians by migrants.
👍 Strengthened the image of the West and the idea that 'Manifest Destiny' was true.	👎 Racism and tension within the settler community due to mass immigration from all over the world.

Impact on Plains Indians

The discovery of gold brought large numbers of migrants onto Indian land. This brought with it serious problems:

- The trails that the migrants used crossed the Black Hills of Dakota, which were sacred to the Plains Indians.
- White settlers brought diseases with them that the Plains Indians had not been exposed to before.
- White settlers had a very different view of how the land should be treated. Mining caused flooding, clogged rivers and killed wildlife. This made it hard for the Plains Indians to survive.

For more on the beliefs of the Plains Indians, see page 9.

Impact on America as a whole

The American government was very pleased with the expansion in California. In 1850, California officially set itself up as a state. By the time the Gold Rush ended in 1856, so many American people lived there that it was unlikely to be attacked or invaded by other countries.

Now try this

Write a short paragraph to explain the negative impact of the Gold Rush on the Plains Indians.

7

Plains Indians: way of life

White settlers first came into contact with the Plains Indians, and their very different way of life, in the 1840s. Life on the Great Plains was very hard and the Plains Indians relied on buffalo and horses to survive.

The Indian nations

A number of Indian nations (or tribes) lived on the Great Plains. These included the Apache, the Cheyenne and the Lakota Sioux. The Plains Indians were not a single group – each nation had its own distinct culture, and there was often conflict between the tribes. However, they shared some key features and beliefs.

White Americans tended to treat the Plains Indians as a single group and ignored the differences between them. This made dealing with the Indian nations more difficult.

The importance of horses

Horses had been brought to America by the Spanish in the 1600s. They gradually became more important to native tribes.

- Plains Indians followed the buffalo through their summer and winter migrations, so horses were vital for transport.
- Hunting on horseback was more efficient than hunting on foot.
- When there was conflict between tribes, horses were used in warfare.
- Plains Indians measured their wealth and status by how many horses they had.

The importance of buffalo

The Plains Indians lived a **nomadic** (travelling) lifestyle centred around the buffalo, which they would follow and hunt throughout the year. The buffalo provided everything the Plains Indians needed. They used every part of the buffalo except for the heart. This was left on the Plains; the Plains Indians believed this gave the herd new life.

Hide – shields, robes, tipi covers, shoes

Fat – soap

Dung – fuel

Sinew – thread, archery bowstrings

Hooves – glue

Intestines – buckets, cooking pots

Coat – blankets, stuffing for saddles, string, gloves

Horn – head pieces, spoons, cups

Skull – used in religious ceremonies

Tongue – brushes

Bones – knives

The ways the Plains Indians used the buffalo

Plains Indians moved their belongings using a 'travois'. This was a triangular platform or net in a V-shaped frame made from two long poles. The travois could be pulled by hand or by horses or dogs. White settlers thought the travois was basic, but it was actually more efficient on the Plains as it was better suited to soft soil and snow than wheels.

As well as tipis, Plains Indians often built circular **lodges**. These were made of tree trunks and woven reeds before being covered with earth. Lodges were usually partially underground. Most of the work was done by women, and a lodge was considered the property of the woman who built it.

The tipi

- ✓ The tipi was a shelter made from buffalo hide.
- ✓ The pyramid shape of the tipi allowed it to withstand the strong winds of the Plains.
- ✓ A tipi was easy to build and take down quickly, fitting with the nomadic lifestyle of the Plains Indians.
- ✓ Tipis were cool in summer and warm in winter, which suited the extreme weather conditions on the Plains.
- ✓ The circular shape was in keeping with the Indians' spiritual beliefs about circles.

For more on the importance of circles to the Plains Indians, see page 9.

Now try this

Write a short paragraph explaining how the Plains Indians' dependence on both horses and buffalo were linked.

Plains Indians: beliefs

The Plains Indians shared certain key beliefs – mainly centred on a respect for nature and the land – and these beliefs brought them into conflict with the white settlers who came west.

The land:
The Plains Indians believed that the land was a living thing and saw it as their mother: living things came from the land and after death they returned to it. They wanted to live in harmony with the land. They thought no person could own it and that farming was disrespectful to the earth.

The spirit world:
The Plains Indians believed that the world was created by the Great Spirit *Wakan Tanka*. During puberty, boys would attend a ceremony to find their **spirit animal** to guide their **visions**. Visions of the spirit world were very important to the Plains Indians' spirituality.

Plains Indians' beliefs

Nature:
The Plains Indians had a deep respect for nature. For them all things had a spirit, including animals, plants, stones and water.

Circles:
Circles were very important to Plains Indians such as the Sioux Nation. They believed that life was a circle from birth through to death. They were respectful of circles in nature, such as the sun and the moon, and the pattern of the seasons. **Tipis** were circular and **Tribal Councils** would sit in a circle as part of this spiritual belief. Dances often took a circular form.

Dances

Sun dance – to thank the Sun for past help and ask for guidance in the future.

Plains Indians performed a number of spiritual **dances** to enter into the spirit world. This painting shows a Sioux war dance.

Buffalo dance – to bring the buffalo to them.

The **Ghost Dance** was invented in 1889 after the Battle of the Little Big Horn. The idea was that the spirits of the dead could be reunited with the spirits of the living and together they could beat the white settlers who were oppressing them.

For more on the Battle of the Little Big Horn, see page 28.

War dance – before going on a raid, tribes would often have up to four days of rituals, designed for them to enter into the spirit world and ask the Spirit for help in the coming battle.

Scalp dance – to celebrate victory in war.

Plains Indians vs white settlers

- Many of the settlers were very religious themselves, mostly Christian. The Plains Indians' ideas about the spirit world and their religion offended the white settlers.
- The white settlers were coming to the Plains intending to own the land, which they believed **'Manifest Destiny'** showed they should live on. This was the opposite of the Plains Indians' idea that the land could not be owned.

- Witnessing things like war dances was very frightening for the white settlers and increased their fear that they were going to be attacked.

You need to be able to identify why these beliefs caused conflict with the white Americans who settled on the Plains.

For more on 'Manifest Destiny', see page 2.

Now try this

Select **three** beliefs of the Plains Indians and explain how these beliefs might bring them into conflict with white settlers.

Plains Indians: tribes and warfare

The Plains Indian **nations** were made up of **tribes**, which in turn were made up of **bands**. Tribal government was based on community spirit and decision making. This seemed very strange to white Americans.

Bands were the smallest unit in a tribe and were often made up of extended families. They were led by chiefs and a council.

Tribes were led by **chiefs**. Chiefs were advised by a tribal council made up of tribal **elders**. The harsh conditions of life on the Plains meant that community spirit was incredibly important.

Laws were not really needed because if people did not work together and do the right things then the bands would not survive.

Leadership

Decisions were made **collaboratively** (everyone discussing and coming to an agreement together).

A chief was usually chosen for his skill as a warrior.

One tribe might have multiple chiefs for different things, such as war and spirituality.

Although a chief's people respected him deeply, he had no power over them.

The white Americans thought that the government should make laws for the good of everyone and make sure they were followed. This was very different to the Plains Indians' tribal way of life. The white settlers could not understand why chiefs could not make their people do as they were told. They did not understand the idea of governing by discussion and community agreement and thought that the Plains Indians simply did not have any kind of government.

Roles within the tribes

You need to be able to compare the lifestyles of the Plains Indians and white settlers.

Even though men could have more than one wife (**polygamy**) this did not mean women were less respected. Polygamy was practised mainly because many young men died in warfare and so there were not enough to look after all the women and children.

Women

Although women could not be chiefs, they held important roles within the tribe. They were responsible for looking after their families, maintaining the **tipi** and processing the parts of the buffalo. Women were greatly respected in Indian society and had special roles in ceremonies such as the Sun dance.

For more on dances, see page 9.

The elderly

Not looking after your parents was seen as a terrible crime and the young took great pride in looking after the elderly. However, when the elderly felt they were no longer useful they would commit **exposure** by voluntarily going off on their own to die in the wilderness.

Children

The Plains Indians cherished their children. There was no formal schooling, but children were prepared for adult life by their relatives. Children were expected to behave well and take part in looking after the family, especially the elderly.

One of the aims of warfare was to steal **horses** and supplies from other tribes or white settlers.

The main tactic was **ambush**.

Fighting was totally **voluntary**.

Counting coup was where a warrior would bravely attempt to hit their enemy with their hand, bow or **coup stick** (a special stick on which the warrior recorded their coup success) and then escape unharmed. This was the highest honour an Indian warrior could achieve.

Warfare and bravery

If a raid looked as if it was not going to be successful, the warriors would **retreat**.

Scalping (removing the skin and hair from an enemy's head to keep as a trophy) was practised in order to stop the enemy from going on to the afterlife, known in some tribes as **The Happy Hunting Ground**.

The Cheyenne had brotherhoods of elite warriors called **Dog Soldiers**.

For more on the conflict caused by the differences in ways of life on the Plains, see page 12.

Now try this

Give **two** differences between the governments of the Plains Indians and the white settlers.

The Permanent Indian Frontier

The American government had always been unsure of what to do about the Plains Indians. The increased migration of white settlers across the Plains, from the 1840s onwards, only made the problem worse.

Early American government policy

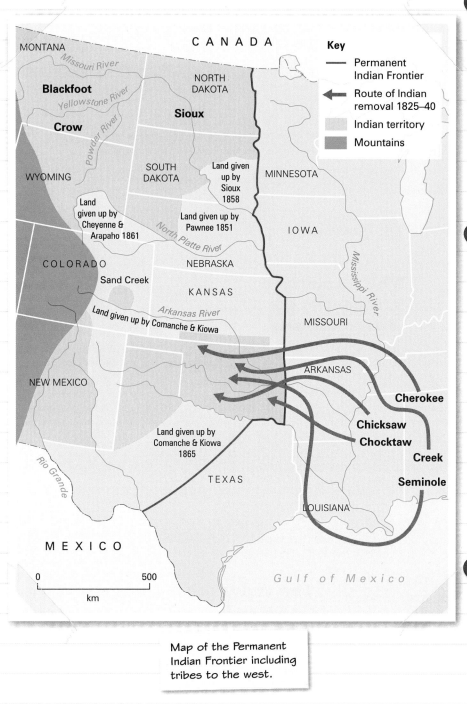

Map of the Permanent Indian Frontier including tribes to the west.

1 1830 Indian Removal Act

This forced Indians living east of the Mississippi to move west, where it was thought they could live separately and without government interference. At this time white Americans and the government thought the Plains were worthless and impossible to settle on. The forced march west became known as the **Trail of Tears** because of the many Cherokees who died during the march.

2 1834 Indian Trade and Intercourse Act

This put in place a **Permanent Indian Frontier** between Indian territory and the Eastern states. The government still believed that the Plains were worthless and could be given to the Indians as '**One Big Reservation**' behind the Permanent Indian Frontier, where the different tribes could live without American government interference. Since many of the removal treaties promised to protect the relocated tribes from white settlers, and since the settlers also demanded protection from the Indian tribes, several forts were built up and down the Frontier.

3 Migration to the West

By the 1840s, the idea that the land beyond the Permanent Indian Frontier was worthless and could be left to the Indians began to change and so did American government policy. The discovery of gold, west of the Frontier, only made these problems worse. More white settlers began to enter and settle on lands west of the Frontier.

Now try this

Write **three** sentences to explain why the American government introduced the Permanent Indian Frontier.

11

Changing relationships

The arrival of white settlers on the Plains by the 1840s changed relationships with the Plains Indians as they now had to live together. Their ways of life were very different and tensions quickly grew.

Attitudes to land

Life on the Great Plains was tough and both settlers and Plains Indians had to work hard to survive. However, unlike the Plains Indians, the white settlers thought that God had given them the right to own the land ('Manifest Destiny').

For more on 'Manifest Destiny', see page 2.

Remember, the relationships between white Americans and the Plains Indians changed because rather than just crossing the Plains to reach places like California, white Americans now began to settle on the Plains in areas where the Plains Indians lived.

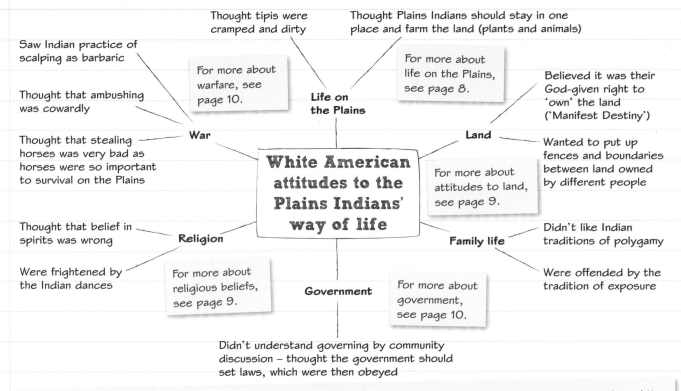

Thought tipis were cramped and dirty

Thought Plains Indians should stay in one place and farm the land (plants and animals)

Saw Indian practice of scalping as barbaric

For more about warfare, see page 10.

Life on the Plains

For more about life on the Plains, see page 8.

Believed it was their God-given right to 'own' the land ('Manifest Destiny')

Thought that ambushing was cowardly

War

Land

Thought that stealing horses was very bad as horses were so important to survival on the Plains

White American attitudes to the Plains Indians' way of life

For more about attitudes to land, see page 9.

Wanted to put up fences and boundaries between land owned by different people

Thought that belief in spirits was wrong

Religion

Family life

Didn't like Indian traditions of polygamy

Were frightened by the Indian dances

For more about religious beliefs, see page 9.

Government

For more about government, see page 10.

Were offended by the tradition of exposure

Didn't understand governing by community discussion – thought the government should set laws, which were then obeyed

The fact that the Plains Indians and white settlers were now living near each other meant that the white settlers saw more of the Plains Indians' lifestyle and so developed deep prejudices against them.

All of this was made worse by the huge increase in numbers of migrants travelling the Oregon Trail in 1849 and 1850 following the discovery of gold in California.

For more on the Gold Rush, see page 7.

Migrants crossing the Plains were alarmed when they saw Indian war parties and assumed they were a threat. This led to more calls for the American government to protect the migrants.

The arrival of the white settlers

The presence of white settlers arriving on the Great Plains affected the lives of the Plains Indians in a number of ways:

- 👎 pressure on food supplies as buffalo herds were disturbed
- 👎 increasing conflict between Indian tribes as food supplies declined
- 👎 tension caused by differences in culture and government.

Now try this

Write a short paragraph to explain why relationships between the white settlers and Plains Indians changed.

Fort Laramie Treaty, 1851

By 1851 the tension between the Plains Indians and white settlers had become a real problem for the American government. The government was keen to expand the settlement of land further westwards but struggled to know how to keep Plains Indians and white settlers apart, so they came up with the **Fort Laramie Treaty**.

Fort Laramie Treaty, 1851
- Each of the Plains tribes would be given its own territory.
- White settlers, travellers and railroad surveyors would be allowed to cross tribal lands safely.
- The American government was allowed to establish forts and roads within Indian territory.
- Selected chiefs from each tribe would negotiate with the American government.
- Plains Indians should pay if their people broke the Treaty.
- The American government promised to protect Plains Indians from white settlers.
- If the Plains Indians stuck to the Treaty, they would be given food and money ($50000 a year).

Remember there were two Fort Laramie Treaties, in 1851 and in 1868. You can revise the Fort Laramie Treaty of 1868 on page 26.

Consequences and difficulties

✓ The Fort Laramie Treaty of 1851 ended the idea of One Big Reservation and instead **concentrated** each tribe within their own lands. Although the Treaty did not create reservations, it was the first step towards them.

✓ The Treaty created a relationship in which the Plains tribes became dependent on the American government for food and money. They were expected to begin behaving in a certain way.

✓ The Treaty was written in English, and without enough interpreters many of the tribes did not fully understand what they had agreed to.

✓ Cultural differences led to misunderstandings. The American government was used to the idea of elected representatives, but Plains tribes had no single leader. Many individual bands still acted as they wanted to.

In the end, the Fort Laramie Treaty failed, and so did the policy of concentration it had introduced.

Many members of the tribes did not even know the Treaty existed.

Those who did know about the Treaty often ignored it and carried on moving into other tribes' territories.

Migrants were supposed to be able to **cross** the Plains Indians' territories without fear of attack but in reality they didn't stick to the official trails and some even settled on land that had been 'given' to the Plains Indians.

The failure of concentration

Cattle drives often went onto Indian territories, causing problems. The discovery of gold in Lakota territory in 1861, and the introduction of railroads, caused further problems.

The American government did nothing to protect the Plains Indians from white settlers, or stop American citizens from causing further conflict.

The promised payments for sticking to the Treaty weren't always made.

Now try this

List **three** outcomes of the Fort Laramie Treaty of 1851.

Indian Wars, 1862–1867: 1

By 1862, the treaties between the Plains Indians and the American government were beginning to break down, and fighting was becoming more common.

Clash of cultures:

- White settlers in the West did not understand the Plains Indians and, because of this, they were afraid of them. White Americans also thought the Plains Indians were not as good as them and should be more like them.

For more on the differences between white settlers and Plains Indians, see page 12.

- **The Homestead Act (1862)** promised white settlers on the Plains 160 acres for free as long as they built a home and farmed the land.
- 'Manifest Destiny' meant that the white settlers believed they should own land. The Plains Indians thought land could not be owned, only looked after.

Broken agreements:

- In the Fort Laramie Treaty of 1851 the Dakota Sioux had agreed to pay off their debts to traders before getting the money the government had promised them. However, they failed to do this so the government refused to pay.
- Some tribes were promised compensation by the government for the poor quality of the land on the reservation they had been moved on to, but the money never came.
- White settlers often ignored the boundaries of reservations and took land that was good for farming.

Reasons for the Indian Wars

Failure of treaties:

- **The Fort Wise Treaty (1861)** had moved the Cheyenne on to the **Sand Creek reservation** but the land was only a thirteenth of the size of the reserve they had before. Some Cheyenne claimed that the treaty never had the approval of most of the tribe, and said that the chiefs were bribed into signing it. Migrants crossing the Plains did not always stick to the agreed trail routes, often straying into land which the Plains Indians used for hunting.
This was against the Fort Laramie Treaty (1851).

For more on the Fort Laramie Treaty of 1851, see page 13.

Poor conditions on the reservations:

- Many tribes who had been moved onto reservations under the policy of concentration faced starvation. This was because of the poor quality of the land they were now living on and the widespread killing of the buffalo they depended on.
- Local traders refused to trade with the Plains Indians so they could not even buy food. Some tribes were reduced to eating grass to try to survive.

For more on concentration, see page 13.

Little Crow's War, 1862

- Little Crow was the chief of a band of Dakota Sioux.
- In 1851, the tribe signed treaties agreeing to move to a reservation in southern Minnesota, giving up 24 million acres of land.
- Land on the reservation was unsuitable for farming, the American government failed to make its promised payments, their crops failed and people began to starve. The government refused to hand over supplies.
- On 17 August 1862 a small Sioux hunting party killed five white settlers. The following day, Little Crow attacked a town, stealing food and supplies and killing over 700 white settlers and soldiers.
- The American government sent in a huge army, and many Sioux surrendered after the **Battle of Wood Lake** on 23 September 1862. 300 Sioux were sentenced to death, and 38 were eventually hanged.

The Cheyenne Uprising, 1863

- After the **Treaty of Fort Laramie**, seven Indian nations (including the Cheyenne) were given a vast territory covering parts of present-day Wyoming, Nebraska, Colorado and Kansas.
- The discovery of gold in Colorado in 1858 caused a gold rush and large numbers of white settlers moved into Indian territory.
- The **Treaty of Fort Wise** in 1861 greatly reduced Cheyenne lands and meant they were living in places that were bad for farming, and far away from the buffalo herds they hunted for survival.
- Many bands of Cheyenne Indians were angry about giving up their lands, and did not think the chiefs who had agreed to it spoke for them.
- In 1863, faced with starvation, some Cheyenne began attacking wagon trains and stealing food and supplies.

Now try this

Give **five** reasons why conflict between white settlers and the Plains Indian tribes became more common from 1862.

Indian Wars, 1862–1867: 2

Confrontations continued to get worse. The **Sand Creek Massacre (1864)** and **Fetterman's Trap (1866)** led to painful consequences for the Plains Indians and their relationship with white settlers and the American government.

Sand Creek Massacre, 1864

Led by their chief, **Black Kettle**, the Cheyenne had attacked wagon trains and stolen food during the Cheyenne Uprising. In response, the American army commanded by **Colonel Chivington** attacked their settlement at Sand Creek on the morning of 29 November 1864. Even though the Plains Indians waved white flags in surrender, Chivington had been given orders to 'kill and destroy' the Plains Indians. More than 150 of them were massacred in a dawn raid, including many of the chiefs who had wanted peace with white Americans. Some, including Black Kettle, escaped to tell other Plains Indians about what had happened.

Red Cloud's War, 1866–1868

In 1863, a miner called John Bozeman established the Bozeman Trail, connecting the Oregon Trail to Montana, where gold had been found. The Bozeman Trail crossed Cheyenne, Sioux and Arapaho hunting grounds, breaking the Treaty of Fort Laramie. Red Cloud, a chief of the Lakota Sioux, led attacks against the travellers that lasted from 1866–1868 and became known as **Red Cloud's War**.

For more on the Fort Laramie Treaty (1851), see page 13.

Fetterman's Trap, 1866

During Red Cloud's War, the American government had established **Fort Phil Kearny** and the Plains Indians began to concentrate their attacks there. On 21 December 1866, a small group of Lakota Sioux, Cheyenne and Arapaho hid near the fort and attacked a party of woodcutters. As the Plains Indians had planned, a group of soldiers under the command of Captain William J. Fetterman left the fort to protect the woodcutters. They were ambushed by a huge force, and all 81 soldiers were killed. The Plains Indians then blocked the route so that no one else could use it. Afterwards, the American government negotiated a second **Fort Laramie Treaty (1868)**. In the Treaty, the government agreed to abandon three forts and the Bozeman Trail, while Red Cloud agreed to move his tribe to a much smaller reservation between the Black Hills of Dakota and the Missouri River.

American army increasingly destroyed Indian lodges, horses, and food supplies.

Despite new treaties, rumours of gold continued to attract white migrants, making further conflict inevitable.

Indian tribes were increasingly forced onto smaller areas of poor-quality land.

Consequences of the Indian Wars

Populations of Plains Indians fell due to disease, famine and war.

By the time of the **Battle of the Little Big Horn (1876)**, many white Americans were demanding the Plains Indians either become like them or be killed.

For more on the Battle of the Little Big Horn, see page 28.

Relationships between Plains Indians and white Americans grew worse, leading to the small reservations policy, the treaties of **Medicine Lodge (1867)** and **Fort Laramie (1868)**, and the **Indian Appropriations Act (1871)**.

Plains Indians felt that the massacre at Sand Creek showed that white Americans could not be trusted.

For more on the Indian Appropriations Act of 1871, see page 27. This is different from the 1851 Act which led to the creation of reservations.

Now try this

Choose **either** the Sand Creek Massacre **or** Fetterman's Trap. Give **two** consequences for the Plains Indians, and their relationships with white settlers and the American government.

North vs South

As the United States grew, the country started to struggle with different ideas about how it should be run. The way the states were **governed**, **slavery** and the **expansion** of the country were all causes of tension.

The federal nature of the American government: This led to power struggles between states and the federal government, often about whether the federal government had the right to stop states from practising slavery.

Each state had a lot of control over its own laws. The states joined together in a **Union**, overseen by the central (**federal**) government which set some laws that were meant to apply to everyone.

Long-term causes of tension

Social and cultural differences between North and South: After the **American Revolutionary War (1775–1783)**, people in the North started to see the **oppression** of slaves as the same as the British oppression of the Americans before the Revolution. As a result, they called for slavery to be abolished (got rid of). This led to a division of the states into **slave states** and **free states**.

In slave states slavery continued to be practised and in **free states** slavery was banned.

Oppression means treating someone cruelly and limiting what they can do.

The debate over secession: Soon, free states started calling for slavery to be banned throughout the Union but slave states did not agree and threatened to secede (leave the Union) if this was the case.

Economic differences between North and South: Slavery was hugely important to the economy of the **agricultural** South where the majority of slaves worked on the plantations. Many of the wealthy businessmen in the **industrial** northern states had made their money by investing in the plantations. However, slavery was not so important to the economy in the North.

The westward expansion of America: This meant that tension over slavery grew as the federal government tried to restrict slavery in new territories applying to join the Union (and become a state). This led to the Missouri Compromise.

For more on the Missouri Compromise, see page 17.

Slavery

Slavery arrived in America in 1619 when a Dutch ship carrying 20 African slaves landed in Virginia. Slaves were a cheap source of labour and worked mainly on the rice and tobacco plantations in the South. In the late 18th century a machine called the **cotton gin** was invented to pick and process cotton. As a result, the South started producing cotton on a large scale to supply the growing textile industry in Britain. This meant that more and more slaves were needed. Between the 1830s and 1860s, support for **abolitionism** grew in strength in the North.

To **abolish** means to put an end to something. **Abolitionism** was the movement to end slavery.

Federal and state government

The USA's federal system of government means that power is divided between federal and state government with some powers shared.

Federal powers
To declare war
To admit new states to the Union
To print money
To make treaties with other countries

Shared powers
To set and collect taxes
To manage law and order
To establish courts

State powers
To agree amendments to the Constitution
To look after local government
To oversee businesses in the state

See page 10 to compare this system with the ways the Plains Indians governed themselves.

Now try this

List **three** reasons for tension between the North and the South.

Growing tensions

Between the 1820s and 1859 problems continued to grow between the North and the South as more territories applied to join the Union. These tensions ultimately led to the outbreak of the Civil War.

Growing tension in the medium term, 1820–1859

Missouri Compromise, 1820
The **Missouri Compromise** was an agreement designed to deal with the spread of slavery into the new territories of the West. It was triggered when Missouri applied to join the Union as a slave state. The compromise drew a line through Louisiana: north of this line slavery would be forbidden, except in Missouri. To balance things out, Maine which was below the line was allowed to join the Union as a free state.

For more on free states and slave states, see page 16.

Nat Turner's Rebellion, 1831
In August 1831, Nat Turner, a black slave, led a slave rebellion which terrified the South. He and six other slaves killed their owners, took horses and weapons and killed 51 white people. The incident made divisions between slave owners and anti-slavery campaigners in the South much deeper and led to harsh laws against slaves.

The Compromise of 1850
The **1850 Compromise** was designed to deal with the issue of slavery in the territories gained by the westward expansion of the USA in the Mexican War (1846–1848). It included laws making it easier for slave owners to get escaped slaves back (such as the **Fugitive Slave Act**). This Compromise also allowed California to join the Union as a free state, created the territory of Utah, and ended the slave trade in Washington, D.C.

For more on Utah, see page 20.

Publication of *Uncle Tom's Cabin* by Harriet Beecher Stowe, 1852

Kansas–Nebraska Act, 1854
As the new states of Kansas and Nebraska were north of the line drawn in the Missouri Compromise, they should have been free states. However, the **Kansas–Nebraska Act** allowed people in these states to decide whether or not to allow slavery themselves. This Act caused the breakdown of the 1850 Compromise, as well as leading to increased tensions and widespread violence.

John Brown's raid on Harpers Ferry, 1859
In October 1859, the **abolitionist** John Brown led an armed raid on the American military weapons store at Harpers Ferry in Virginia. The raid was supposed to be the first stage in a plan to set up a refuge for freed slaves in the mountains of Virginia. However, Brown was captured, convicted of treason and hanged. The raid made white Southern fears of slave rebellions worse and greatly increased tension between Northern and Southern states.

It might seem as if arguments over slavery were the only cause of the Civil War but the reality was more complicated. It was the combination of all these long-term issues that made the tense situation even worse from the 1820s onwards.

Uncle Tom's Cabin

Uncle Tom's Cabin tells the story of some Southern slaves and was written to persuade people that slavery should end. The novel came out two years after the Fugitive Slave Act and showed many people the true horrors of the Southern slave system. The book had a huge impact on people's opinions about slavery, and made tensions between slave states and free states worse. Some historians even think that the book contributed to the outbreak of the Civil War.

A poster advertising *Uncle Tom's Cabin* by Harriet Beecher Stowe. It claims it is 'the greatest book of the age' and has sold 270 000 volumes (copies).

Now try this

Write **three** sentences explaining how the poster for *Uncle Tom's Cabin* helps you understand the causes of the Civil War.

Outbreak of war

The election of President Lincoln in 1860 was deeply unpopular in the South. When South Carolina seceded the Union in the same year, other Southern states followed and war soon broke out.

Short-term causes of the Civil War, 1860–1861

New political parties
By 1854, a new political party called the **Republicans** had formed in America. The party was made up of: **Northerners** who had left the **Whig Party** which no longer existed; some **Democrats** who didn't like slavery or the concept of 'Manifest Destiny'; and a few members of the strongly Protestant and anti-immigration **Know Nothing Party**.

For more on 'Manifest Destiny', see page 2.

President of the United States of America
The election of the strongly anti-slavery president **Abraham Lincoln** was deeply unpopular in the South and they could see no other option than secession.

Secession of South Carolina
Southern States had been threatening to secede if the Republicans and their anti-slavery candidate won the White House. South Carolina was the first state to secede and, by the time Lincoln was **inaugurated** as president in March 1861, seven Southern states had seceded and formed the **Confederate States of America**.

President of the Confederacy
When the Southern states began seceding, pro-slavery Southerner Jefferson Davis was chosen to be President of the Confederacy in February 1861. In November 1861, Davis was elected to a six-year term under a new Confederate constitution.

The Battle of Fort Sumter
In April 1861, the first shots of the Civil War were fired at Fort Sumter in South Carolina. Confederate forces rowed to the fort (in boats rowed by slaves) and demanded that the Union forces leave. When they refused the Confederates opened fire.

An American president does not start their role until they are formally inaugurated, which involves a ceremony to mark the beginning of their term. This usually takes place 2–4 months after the election.

Abraham Lincoln

Abraham Lincoln was born on 12 February 1809, in Hardin County, Kentucky. Before his career in politics, he was a lawyer.

During the 1860 election campaign, he presented himself as a man of the people and an opponent of wealthy slave owners. He promised to give more land to settlers in the West and stop the expansion of slavery. He became known as 'Honest Abe' and took over the presidency in 1861, shortly before the start of the Civil War. After a difficult second election he was re-elected in 1864 but he was then assassinated in April 1865.

Jefferson Davis

Jefferson Davis was the first and only President of the Confederate States of America. He was born and grew up in the South and was a firm believer that slavery was both right and important for the economy. Davis had experience as a soldier as well as a politician and did not actually want to be president, but he was very popular because he was so dedicated to the Confederate cause. He became unpopular after promoting unpopular leaders and a series of Confederate losses. He was captured by Union troops in May 1865, a few weeks after the Confederates surrendered.

Now try this

You will need to refer to pages 16–18 for your answer.

Draw a three-column table with these headings linked to the American Civil War: Long-term causes; Medium-term causes; Short-term causes. Under each heading, list **three** examples. These could be issues or events. Try to give dates for any events you list.

Impacts of the war

The Civil War changed the lives of thousands of ordinary people. The social and economic impacts of the American Civil War on civilian populations were huge.

What were the social and economic impacts of the American Civil War on civilians?

Industry and agriculture

- Large armies trampled across farms in the South and the border states between the North and South, confiscating animals and farm buildings for the war effort.
- The industrial North had a big advantage over the South because it already had factories and railroads, whereas the South had been an agricultural economy. As a result, the North was able to produce supplies for soldiers and civilians more easily than the South could.
- The agriculture in the North used more machines than the South, where the land was mainly worked by slaves. As a result, the war and the end of slavery had less of an impact on agriculture in the North than in the South.
- The South struggled as they had no real currency and inflation was very high. As the war went on the money printed in the South became worth less and less.

The spreading of news

- The invention of the telegraph meant that news of the war could reach the North faster than ever before. As a result, people were more aware of the horrors of war.
- Newspapers carrying news of the war, including pictures, were more widespread than before.

A photograph of dead soldiers after the Battle of Gettysburg, 1863. For the first time, newspapers were able to show the horrors of war to those who lived far away from any actual fighting.

Changing role of women

- The Civil War pushed women in the North and South into public life in a way that had been unthinkable before.
- In both the North and the South, thousands of women worked as nurses or set up societies to try to supply troops with everything they needed.
- In the South, women – whose children were starving – sometimes organised protests against the conditions they were living in.

Living in a war zone

- Life was hugely disrupted for families in both the North and the South, especially if **conscription** forced their husbands, brothers and sons into military service.
- The North blockaded (stopped goods entering or leaving) the South, which caused shortages as Southerners could not produce everything they needed or buy in extra supplies from the North.
- Many people in the South, especially women and children, left homes in communities which had become occupied and were now battlegrounds. This created a large refugee population.
- **Guerrilla warfare** raged in many Southern states. This was frightening and disruptive for people living in the occupied areas.
- Southern towns were often placed under martial law (control by the army) with restrictions to people's rights and daily lives.

Guerrilla warfare is where small, unofficial groups use surprise tactics, such as ambushes and sabotage, against larger forces.

Now try this

How were Americans affected by the ways they got information about the Civil War? Write a short paragraph to explain your thoughts, using the photograph as well as the information above to help you.

Mountain Meadows Massacre, 1857

Between 1848 and 1896 the Mormons and the American government had to work out the relationship between Utah and the rest of the Union. They needed to come to terms, in other words, reach an agreement.

For more on the Mormons, see pages 3–4.

Coming to terms with the Mormons

1848: Handover of Salt Lake to the USA
The Mexican–American War broke out in 1846 over who owned Texas. It ended in an American victory in 1848, and Mexico handed over a huge amount of territory to the USA – including the Salt Lake Valley. The Mormons, who had settled in the Salt Lake Valley in 1847, were now back in the USA and old tensions returned. Under the direction of Brigham Young, the Mormons asked the American government to recognise their lands as an independent state called 'Deseret'.

1850: Utah established as a territory
The USA refused to allow an independent Deseret, but instead established the territory of Utah, appointing Brigham Young as governor. Utah was not a state, so it did not have the right to make its own laws on matters such as marriage or property. Mormon settlements spread quickly and the government in the East began to worry about the spread of Mormonism.

1857: Mountain Meadows Massacre
In 1857, the government sent troops to Utah to force Young to follow American laws. The result was the Mountain Meadows Massacre. The Massacre almost led to America and the Mormons declaring war as relations between them were already poor.

1857–1858: The Utah War
Apart from Mountain Meadows, there was an armed standoff between the American government and the Mormons. Eventually an agreement was negotiated about how Utah would relate to the rest of the Union. The Mormon rebels were pardoned in exchange for accepting the authority of the American government.

1890: The Mormon *Manifesto*
Wilford Woodruff, President of the Mormon Church, issued his *Manifesto*. This formally ended the practice of polygamy in an attempt to compromise with the American government.

In 1896, Utah was admitted to the Union as a state.

The Mountain Meadows Massacre, 1857

Believing the American military were on their way to Utah to attack them, the Mormons began to prepare for war. A group of Danites (Mormon militia) led by John D Lee persuaded a group of Pauite Indians to join in an attack on the Baker–Fancher wagon train carrying migrants on their way to California.

After a five-day siege, the attackers lured 120 people, including men, women and children, away from the camp by pretending they would see them safely out of Utah. They then murdered them. The possessions of the dead were auctioned off and the youngest children, who had been left alive, were taken in by local families.

In their hurry to bury the bodies the Danites left some exposed and were found out. John D Lee was the only person ever tried and executed for the crime.

Cartoon from an American newspaper of 1882, entitled 'Mormonism in Utah – the cave of despair', warning European migrants of the dangers awaiting them in Utah. The sign on the left of the picture reads 'Mountain Meadows' and the label at the back reads 'Salt Lake'.

Now try this

Write a short paragraph to explain what the cartoon above tells you about the worsening relations between Mormons and other Americans at this time.

Reunifying the nation

After the North's victory in the American Civil War, the American government needed to bring the nation back together and show that federal government was stronger than state government. They did this by passing a number of key pieces of **legislation** (laws) to abolish slavery and protect African Americans.

Legislation, 1865–1870

 Timeline

1865 The 13th Amendment abolishes slavery.

The 13th Amendment abolished slavery unless it was punishment for a crime.

The Civil Rights Act of 1866 declared all people who were born in the USA were citizens and had full legal rights. It also made it illegal to deny someone these rights under federal law.

1866 The Civil Rights Act of 1866.

1868 The 14th Amendment.

The 14th Amendment gave equal rights and citizenship to African Americans and slaves who had been set free after the American Civil War.

1870 The 15th Amendment.

The 15th Amendment protected the right of **all** American citizens to vote in elections, and made it illegal to deny someone this right because of their race or status as a former slave.

1870 The Civil Rights Act of 1870.

The Civil Rights Act 1870 was also known as the Enforcement Act and was designed to reinforce the 15th Amendment by bringing in federal criminal penalties for anyone trying to prevent African Americans voting or threatening them in any way.

The 13th, 14th and 15th Amendments are known as the **Reconstruction Amendments** because they happened during a period called the **Reconstruction of the South** after the Confederacy lost the Civil War.

For more on the Reconstruction of the South, see page 22.

Acts of terror by groups such as the **Ku Klux Klan** undermined the Civil Rights Acts of 1866 and 1870.

A Ku Klux Klan member aims his rifle into an African-American home. Despite federal laws, such as the Civil Rights Acts of 1866 and 1870 and the 14th and 15th Amendments, violence against African Americans was still common.

Now try this

Write a short paragraph to explain how effective the Civil Rights Act of 1866 was in protecting African Americans. Use the picture above as well as the information in the timeline to help you.

Reconstruction in the South

The Reconstruction Era is the name given to the period 1865–1877. During this time, the American government struggled to rebuild the South and to bring the Southern states back into the Union.

Presidential Reconstruction, 1865–1866

President Johnson, a Democrat, thought that the Southern states should still govern themselves despite their involvement in the Civil War.

- Land confiscated by the Union army and given to freed slaves was returned to the original Confederate owners.
- Southern states were allowed to govern themselves as long as they did not allow slavery and they paid off their war debts.
- Many Southern states used this as an opportunity to pass **Black Codes** which upset many Northerners.
- Violence against black Americans was still a problem.

For more on Black Codes, see page 23.

For more on the legislation of 1865–1870, see page 21.

Carpetbaggers

After **1865**, a number of Northerners moved to the South hoping to profit from the poor economic situation there. They were known as **carpetbaggers** because they often used cheap bags made from carpet fabric. They planned to buy or rent land in the South that used to be profitable but would now struggle without slave labour.

To begin with they were welcomed for investing in the region to help it get back on its feet after the Civil War. However, as time went on many Southerners felt carpetbaggers were trying to get rich on the back of their struggles. The carpetbaggers also had a lot of influence in Southern politics with 60 of them elected to Congress as Republicans.

Radical Reconstruction, 1866–1876

In 1866 the Republicans in Congress took charge of Reconstruction:

- They passed the Reconstruction Acts of 1867 placing the South under military rule.
- Southern states had to agree to the 14th Amendment giving freed slaves equal protection to white Americans before they would be allowed to rejoin the Union.
- The Republicans also made the Southern states agree to the 15th Amendment guaranteeing freed slaves the right to vote.
- For the first time, black Americans won elections to government positions.

Reconstruction Acts of 1867

Under these Acts the ten Southern states were divided into five military districts. The army was put in charge with two main purposes:

- to protect life and property
- to organise the political situation.

The victorious North now wanted the South to live by the same social and political standards as they did: black and white Americans living as equals and not using violence to settle disputes.

Re-admission into the Union

By **1870**, all of the Confederate states had been allowed to rejoin the Union. They could do this once they had met the necessary requirements, which included abolition of slavery, swearing their loyalty to the Union, and allowing freedmen (freed slaves) to register to vote. Many historians have argued that the main concern of Northerners during the Reconstruction Era was to make sure that black Americans had the right to vote.

End of military rule in the South

As part of the **Compromise of 1876–1877**, President Hayes agreed that the South was once again under Democrat control and the last soldiers were pulled out of the South.

Now try this

Write a short paragraph to explain **one** key difference between Presidential Reconstruction and Radical Reconstruction.

Freed slaves

The victory of the Northern States (the Union) in the Civil War **emancipated** (set free) around four million slaves. The American government had to manage how to include these people in American society.

Impact of emancipation

Freeing the slaves meant huge changes to the culture of the South and these were not popular with many Americans.

- It destroyed the plantation-based economy of the South, which now struggled to operate without slave labour.

- Poverty became a real problem for both freed slaves and many white former plantation owners who were struggling financially after they lost slave labour. This was made worse by a series of failed crops.

- In the 1870s, **white supremacy** (the belief that white Americans were superior to everyone else) became common in the South.

- A financial crash in 1874 made the economic problems in the South even worse. This made the Republicans unpopular and the Democrats took over the South again.

Political:

- The **Freedmen's Bureau** was set up to provide help for freed slaves and very poor white Southerners. However, President Johnson was against it, saying it was too sympathetic towards the freed slaves.

- The North was determined that the freed slaves should have the right to vote. This was finally given to them in the 15th Amendment.

- Under **Radical Reconstruction**, black Americans were elected to government for the first time.

> **The situation of freed slaves**

Social:

- There was now a huge refugee population of freed black slaves who had no employment, housing or basic supplies such as food.

- Violence against the freed slaves was common after the war ended and before the military took charge.

- Black Codes were designed to restrict the freedoms of freed slaves to make sure they were still going to be the main source of labour in the South.

- Radical Reconstruction was not popular and many white Southern groups such as the Ku Klux Klan turned to violence against black Americans and their supporters.

- Many former slaves moved north to look for work in factories. Black populations began to grow in cities like New York and Chicago.

Economic:

- Many freed slaves thought that they were entitled to land and to begin with they were given some.

- Much of this land had been taken from Confederates but it was quickly taken back and given to its original owners.

- White Americans were reluctant to sell land to black Americans, so most former slaves had to rent or work for wages on plantations. Many paid their rent with a share of their crop – they became known as **sharecroppers**.

- As time went on and conditions got worse, freed slaves started to complain that their wages weren't being paid. Their white employers said it was because the harvest had failed but really many saw it as an opportunity to return to how things had been before.

- Poverty was a real problem both in black American and in some white American communities. This led to high levels of debt.

Now try this

Give **two** key ways in which life changed for slaves after their emancipation, and **two** key ways in which it stayed the same.

Reasons for going west

Before the Civil War, most people who went west were looking for land. However, this changed both during and after the Civil War. Reasons for going west now included the building of the railroads, opportunities for freed slaves, and the government's new promotion of 'Manifest Destiny'.

You need to be able to identify which of these factors are **push** factors and which are **pull** factors.

Push and Pull factors

Economic	• **PUSH:** Freed slaves moved west to escape economic problems in the South after the Civil War. • **PULL:** The **Homestead Act, 1862** offered free land to people who could never have afforded it in the South or East. • **PULL:** The railroad companies helped people move west by offering them discounted travel, accommodation until their homesteads were built, free land, and reduced taxes. • **PULL:** Former soldiers moved west to start new lives after the Civil War.
Religious	• **PUSH:** A lot of migrants came from Europe after the Civil War looking for religious freedom – such as Dutch Protestants, Irish Catholics and Jews from Eastern Europe. • **PULL:** The railroad companies had departments dedicated to encouraging European settlers to come west.
Political	• **PULL:** Federal laws promised free land through the Homestead Act, 1862. • **PULL:** The government was again promoting 'Manifest Destiny'. • **PULL:** To encourage new railroads in the West, the American government gave railroad companies the land for two miles either side of the tracks, which they then offered to settlers. This led to huge sales campaigns for people to 'Go West!'. • **PULL:** The government encouraged publicity campaigns about how life in the West was attractive and would make settlers rich. • **PULL:** Government policy of moving the Plains Indians onto reservations gave people more confidence that they would be safe when moving west.
Other	• **PUSH:** Increasing violence from groups like the Ku Klux Klan made life dangerous for freed slaves in the South so moving west was very attractive. • **PULL:** Early settlers to the West after the Civil War sent back stories that life was full of opportunity and freedom. This encouraged more people to migrate.

For more on the South's economic problems, see pages 22–23.

For more on 'Manifest Destiny', see page 2.

For more on this policy, see pages 26–32.

Some historians now question how many freed slaves actually went west. They argue that some states had laws discouraging black people from settling in them.

Before the Civil War, Southern states tried to stop the government encouraging settlement in the West.

After Southern states withdrew from the Union, the American government passed laws like the Pacific Railroad Act, 1862.

The Acts allowed huge railroads to be built across America.

The railroads

New railroads could take settlers and supplies to the West more quickly and cheaply.

The railroads meant Western farmers could send their produce east for sale.

By 1880, railroads had helped settle people on around 200 million acres in the West.

Now try this

After the Civil War, there was an increase in people moving west. Write **three** sentences explaining how the railroads contributed to this increase.

Homesteaders

Homesteaders faced a number of problems in settling in the West, such as the climate, natural disasters and the unsuitability of existing machinery, crops and landholdings. As a result, they had to adapt their way of life to survive. The American government also had to come up with solutions to support homesteaders – such as developing the railroads.

Problems and solutions

Problem	Explanation	Solution
Lack of timber (not many trees on the Plains)	There was nothing to build houses with.	People built 'sod' houses made from blocks of earth.
	There was nothing to make fences to contain cattle and protect crops from animals.	In 1874, barbed wire was invented, which was quick and cheap to erect and did not require the use of much wood.
	There was nothing to use for cooking and heating.	Women collected dried buffalo and cattle dung, which was used for fuel.
Lack of water	There was low rainfall and few rivers or lakes.	Drills were developed to find underground water, then wind pumps were built to bring it to the surface.
Climate	The weather was unpredictable, sometimes including strong winds and violent storms. Winters were very cold, and summers were very warm and dry.	Sod houses were well insulated and therefore cool in the summer, and warm in the winter.
Hard, arid land (crops wouldn't grow)	The soil was heavy and difficult to break. Ploughs often broke going through deep-rooted grass or work was done by hand.	Mass-produced and stronger machinery from eastern factories helped cultivate land more easily.
	Low rainfall prevented growth of crops like maize and wheat, which farmers were used to growing in the East.	New techniques like dry farming (which conserved rainwater) were used. Migrants from Russia used Turkey Red wheat, which thrived on the Plains.
Natural disasters (prairie fires and pests that destroyed crops)	Pests, such as grasshoppers, could destroy a whole season's crop. Fire spread quickly and burned everything.	There were no solutions. Homesteaders could be bankrupted by such disasters.
Land holdings were too small	The 160 acres allocated in the Homestead Act could not support the average family.	The **Timber Culture Act 1873** let homesteaders have another 160 acres if they promised to plant trees on half of it. The **Desert Land Act 1877** let settlers buy 640 acres of desert land cheaply.
Disease and lack of medical care (people were often ill)	Sod houses were hard to keep clean and had no sanitation.	Women cared for the sick, using their own remedies. As communities grew, doctors arrived.
Lack of education	Most homesteads were too far from towns with schools.	Women taught the young. As communities grew, single female teachers arrived and schools developed.
Isolation	Life was lonely and tough on the Plains.	Railroads improved travel and brought much-needed supplies and new machinery to homesteaders.

Now try this

In a short paragraph, explain **one** way in which the government helped homesteaders to solve a problem they faced when farming the Plains.

Small reservations policy

The American government now set out to resolve 'the Indian Problem' with its **small reservations policy**. This was set out in the treaties of **Medicine Lodge (1867)** and **Fort Laramie (1868)**.

Resolving 'the Indian problem'

By 1865 attitudes towards the West and the Plains Indians had changed significantly. The American government had previously agreed that the Plains should be 'one big reservation' on which the Plains Indians could be left alone to continue their traditional way of life. Now the American government created a fully developed reservation system, splitting up the large Indian tribes and forcing them to live on small reservations.

By 1865 the Plains Indians had become a huge threat to the development of the West, standing in the way of new communication lines and railroad-building programmes. In addition, a growing number of white Americans were settling on the Plains and saw the Plains Indians as a threat.

For more on the Permanent Indian Frontier, see page 11.

The American government was encouraged to adopt a reservation system by **Humanitarians**. For more on this, see page 27.

Medicine Lodge Treaties, 1867

✓ The treaties finally ended the idea of One Big Reservation. Instead the Southern Plains Indians had to move to a much smaller reservation in Oklahoma.

✓ Plains Indians living outside the reservation would be forced onto the reservation by the military, using violence if necessary.

✓ The Plains Indians would be encouraged to give up their traditional ways and expected to **assimilate** with (become like) white Americans.

✓ The government would 'support' this assimilation by setting up boarding schools for Indian children and agricultural programmes to teach people how to farm.

Fort Laramie Treaty, 1868

✓ The American government agreed to close the Bozeman Trail and abandon its forts across the West.

For more on the Bozeman Trail, see page 15.

✓ Red Cloud and the Sioux realised they could not beat the American government in the long term and agreed to move to a small reservation in the Black Hills of South Dakota.

✓ In return, the American government promised to supply the Sioux on the reservation with food and medicine.

Don't forget there were **two** Fort Laramie treaties, one in 1851 and one in 1868. For more on the Fort Laramie Treaty of 1851, see page 13.

From homelands to reservations

Indian homelands (in blue) in 1862, before the Medicine Lodge Treaties of 1867 (reservations in red)

Indian reservations (in red) in 1876, after the Fort Laramie Treaty of 1868 (Indian homelands in blue)

Now try this

Write a short paragraph to explain why American government policy towards the Plains Indians changed after 1865.

Attitudes and adaptations

The American people's opinions were divided between those who wanted to exterminate the Indian population, and those who wanted to move them out of the way. The Plains Indians constantly tried to adapt to these attitudes in order to survive.

Exterminators vs humanitarians

Exterminators were white Americans who thought that the government should not be making treaties with the Plains Indians. Instead they thought all the Plains Indians should simply be exterminated (killed). They were angry that Plains Indians were attacking white settlers and the American military. This anger grew stronger during the **Indian Wars of 1875–85**, with events like the Battle of the Little Big Horn.

Humanitarians did not want to fight with the Plains Indians and wanted them moved onto reservations instead. They thought that fighting them would only make things worse, causing the Plains Indians to fight back harder.

Humanitarians often accused exterminators, such as Lieutenant Colonel Custer and General Sherman, of deliberately provoking the Plains Indians into violent conflict.

How did the Plains Indians adapt?

Most Plains Indians realised they could not beat the American government in the long term and agreed to the conditions of treaties like Medicine Lodge in exchange for much needed supplies. However, conditions on the reservations were so poor that starvation and terrible diseases were common.

For more about life on the reservations, see page 30.

As a result, many Plains Indians – such as Sioux Chief Red Cloud, who signed the Laramie Treaty of 1868 – agreed to humiliating conditions such as sending their children away to boarding schools where they would be taught how to be more American.

Indian Appropriations Act, 1871
- This said that Indian nations and tribes were no longer an independent power.
- It took away the need for the government to try to make treaties with them.
- It brought Indian affairs under the control of the government.

General William T Sherman

General William T Sherman was a Civil War leader who was stationed in the West at the end of the Civil War to protect railroad workers. Sherman was an **exterminator**. He was part of the team who negotiated the Fort Laramie Treaty of 1868 and used the opportunity to push for harsher treatment of the Plains Indians.

For more on the Fort Laramie Treaty of 1868, see page 26.

The extermination of the buffalo

One of the ways the American government tried to encourage the Plains Indians to assimilate and live like white Americans was to kill all of the buffalo. This meant that the Plains Indians could no longer rely on hunting them for food, clothes and other supplies. Millions of buffalo were killed and their bones used for fertiliser. By 1890 hardly any buffalo were left on the Plains.

For more on how the Plains Indians used buffalo, see page 8.

Now try this

Give **one** event or policy that reflects the ideas of the exterminators and **one** that reflects the ideas of the humanitarians.

Little Big Horn: growing tensions and battle

In 1876, the 7th Cavalry, led by George Custer, was defeated by Plains Indian warriors in the Battle of the Little Big Horn. The battle was the result of growing tensions over gold found in Sioux hunting grounds and the reservations policy.

Background to the battle

In 1873, the building of the Northern Pacific Railroad approached Lakota Sioux hunting grounds in Dakota.

> The Lakota Sioux – led by Crazy Horse and Sitting Bull – resisted attempts by the American government to move them onto small reservations so tensions were already high.

Thousands of prospectors headed for the Black Hills of Dakota where gold had been discovered.

> By being in the Black Hills, Custer and his men were clearly breaking the Fort Laramie Treaty of 1868.

Sioux warriors attacked prospectors camped in Indian hunting grounds. The American government offered to buy the Black Hills from the Sioux, but the Sioux refused.

> Sitting Bull and Crazy Horse were joined by large numbers of Sioux, Arapaho and Cheyenne warriors who believed the government had betrayed them.

Bands of Sioux warriors – led by **Sitting Bull** and **Crazy Horse** – continued to attack prospectors. In December 1875, the American government declared that the Sioux had broken the Fort Laramie Treaty of 1868 and ordered the Sioux to return to their small reservations.

> The Plains Indians were given 60 days to return to their reservations but the winter conditions meant they could not travel.

President Grant declared that any Plains Indians outside the reservations could be attacked. By the spring of 1876, 10 000 Plains Indians had reached the camp at the Little Big Horn River. Among them were around 3000 warriors, armed with rifles.

The Battle of the Little Big Horn, June 1876

Custer was ordered to scout out the situation and wait for reinforcements. Instead he divided his 600 men into three groups to attack on three sides. He personally led 200 men into the valley to attack the Plains Indians on the northern side.

General Sheridan was sent to defeat the Plains Indians. The American armies gathered at the Yellowstone River.

Lieutenant Colonel George Custer, leading the 7th Cavalry, ignored his instructions to march around the Wolf Mountains, hoping to be first to the Plains Indians' camp.

Custer's Last Stand, 25 June 1876

Custer's men were outnumbered and quickly defeated by the Plains Indian force, led by Crazy Horse.

> Crazy Horse was a skilled warrior and commander: within one hour, Custer and all of his men were dead.

Now try this

In a short paragraph, summarise the events leading up to the Battle of the Little Big Horn.

Little Big Horn: responsibilities and consequences

The Battle of the Little Big Horn in 1876 transformed American government policy towards the Plains Indians. After their defeat by the Sioux, the American government and the American public decided they were no longer going to try to come to peaceful agreements with the Plains Indians.

Custer:

- Custer ignored his instructions to make camp and wait for reinforcements, choosing instead to attack with only 600 cavalrymen (soldiers on horses).
- Custer had marched his men through the Wolf Mountains on the way to the valley of the Little Big Horn instead of going round them as ordered. As a result, his troops and horses were tired before the battle began.
- Some historians have suggested that Custer was arrogant and had expected the Sioux warriors to run away. However, Crazy Horse and his men were experienced and fearless warriors.
- He refused an offer of Gatling guns (early machine guns) fearing it would slow his men down, and claiming that they could face anything without them.

Bad luck:

- It was an approved army tactic to divide your forces, but it left Custer and the 200 men he led into the valley hugely outnumbered.
- Custer attacked quickly because he was afraid his forces had been discovered by Sioux in the area. In fact, these Sioux were returning to their reservations, and did not alert the other Plains Indians to Custer's presence.

Why did Custer lose at Little Big Horn?

Custer's commanders:

- The information Custer had from his superiors was incomplete: he had no idea how many men he would be fighting or what they were armed with.

Custer's subordinates:

- Major Reno and Captain Benteen used standard army procedure and failed to consider the Indians' tactics of stealth and ambush.

Plains Indians:

- Custer's forces were hugely outnumbered by the Indian warriors.
- The Plains Indians were simply better warriors.
- It is possible that the Indian scouts Custer employed led him to the enemy. This had happened at the Battle of Washita in 1868, where Custer 'forgot' his orders and massacred 103 Plains Indians – mainly women and children.

Little Big Horn: consequences

- ✓ Public opinion quickly changed and there was no longer support for the policy of trying to reach peaceful agreements with the Plains Indians.
- ✓ People now saw the Plains Indians as a real threat.
- ✓ American government policy altered to crushing Indian resistance.
- ✓ Indirectly, the battle led to the Dawes Act, the **Ghost Dance** movement and the massacre at **Wounded Knee**.
- ✓ To some, Custer was a war hero – mostly because his wife worked hard to present this image.
- ✓ Others, such as President Grant, placed the blame for the defeat firmly on Custer.

Changes in government policy

- ✓ Treaties which had been made with the Plains Indians in the past were ignored after the Battle of the Little Big Horn.
- ✓ Plains Indians were moved onto even smaller reservations, in worse conditions.
- ✓ The military made great efforts to keep the Plains Indians on their reservations, often by starving them, or stealing their horses and ammunition.
- ✓ Forts were built across the West.
- ✓ The government exploited the Plains Indians' need for food and supplies to get them finally to give up land.

Victory at the Little Big Horn became seen by the Plains Indians as a **pyrrhic victory** (a victory achieved at too great a cost).

Now try this

In a short paragraph, explain who you think was mainly responsible for the defeat of the 7th Cavalry at the Battle of the Little Big Horn. Give **three** reasons in your answer.

The Dawes Act, 1887

After the **Battle of the Little Big Horn**, white Americans no longer supported the idea that the Plains Indians could continue their old ways of life. The American government set about changing the way the Plains Indians lived once and for all with the **Dawes Act**.

Poor land: The Plains Indians were given the land that white Americans didn't want. It was harder to farm and this meant that crops failed.

Overcrowding: There was not enough food for everyone and overcrowding led to deadly outbreaks of diseases brought by white people such as smallpox and measles.

Conflict: Reservations often contained different bands and tribes who had been at war with each other before being moved to the reservation.

Reservation life before 1887

Culture: Plains Indians on the reservations were expected to wear non-Indian clothing and give up their traditional cultural practices.

Religion: Christian missionaries tried to persuade the Plains Indians to give up their spiritual ways and become Christians. They were also encouraged to speak English.

Power: In the early 1880s, the government tried to **break the power system** of the Plains Indians. They set up **councils** that they then controlled through threats and bribes.

Smaller reservations: The size of reservations had become much smaller and it became impossible for the Plains Indians to continue their nomadic way of life.

Impact of the Dawes Act

The Dawes Act, 1887

✓ The Act split up reservations into small units of land known as allotments.

✓ These allotments were given to individual tribesmen to farm with around 160 acres for each adult and 60 acres for each child.

✓ The Act changed the legal status of Plains Indians from members of tribes to American individuals like everyone else.

✓ Plains Indians who accepted the small units of land were allowed to become American citizens.

✓ The Act created state-funded boarding schools where Indian children were forced to go to learn to be more American.

The Plains Indians now had to farm like homesteaders on small farms. They did not have the necessary skills and their land was too small to grow everything they needed to survive. As a result many Indian families starved.

Plains Indians now had to live in small family groups which was considered to be 'more American' and aimed to end tribal loyalties.

The land was held by the government for 25 years, during which time the Plains Indians had to prove they were capable of farming the land. Otherwise the government would take it back and sell it to someone else, usually a white settler.

Indian children were sent away to schools to help them integrate into white American culture. They were taught that Indian culture was backwards and uncivilised, and were punished if they spoke their native language or joined in anything from their native culture like dances or rituals.

President Cleveland thought that he was doing the right thing by getting the Plains Indians off the isolated reservations they had been moved to as a result of previous laws. He argued that their quality of life would improve and that the moves would help them to assimilate into white American culture more quickly.

Now try this

Give **two** ways in which the Dawes Act reduced the feeling that Plains Indians were a threat to white Americans.

Wounded Knee, 1890

By 1877 Indian resistance to the American government was over. However, American military harassment of the Sioux continued until 1890 when the army massacred 150–300 Lakota Sioux at Wounded Knee.

Events at Wounded Knee

In **1889**, the **Ghost Dance Spiritual Movement** began.

On **15 December 1890**, Indian Reservation Police tried to arrest Chief Sitting Bull, wrongly thinking that he was a Ghost Dancer and about to lead a rebellion. Sitting Bull refused to go quietly and in the fight that followed he was shot dead. This greatly angered his followers, who fled south to join another Lakota Sioux Chief, Big Foot.

On **29 December 1890**, the American army 7th Cavalry caught up with Big Foot and Sitting Bull's followers at Wounded Knee Creek, demanded their surrender and began to disarm them. They refused and, as a result of the tension, a fight broke out between a Plains Indian and an American soldier. Shots were fired and in the massacre that followed the 7th Cavalry slaughtered 150–300 Plains Indians, half of them women and children, while around 25 American soldiers died. The remaining Plains Indians surrendered.

The Ghost Dance movement

In 1890 a Paiute Indian named **Wovoka** claimed to have had a vision telling him that the Plains Indians had angered the **Great Spirit**. The Great Spirit was angry because they had abandoned their traditional ways of life, which had led to their defeat and the move to the reservations.

Wovoka claimed that if they danced the sacred Ghost Dance and rejected white American ways, the Great Spirit would bring back to life all dead Plains Indians, help them to defeat the white people and restore their traditional way of life.

The Ghost Dance movement quickly became popular on the reservations and this deeply worried the American government. President Harrison sent the military into the reservations to stop the Ghost Dance movement.

 Some historians have suggested that the 7th Cavalry were actually just taking revenge for the defeat at the Little Big Horn.

Reactions to Wounded Knee

- White Americans were relieved that the Ghost Dance movement had been ended.

- The events were immediately portrayed by newspapers and the army as a battle and the soldiers who took part were praised for their actions and the Plains Indians condemned for attacking them.

- The events at Wounded Knee confirmed American public opinion that the Plains Indians were wild savages and that those who could not be controlled should be killed.

- The massacre at Wounded Knee was the last major violent confrontation in the clash between the American army and the Plains Indians.

Engraving from a newspaper at the time of Wounded Knee. The newspapers exaggerated Indian violence and this encouraged public hostility towards the Indian nations.

After the massacre at Wounded Knee the American government announced that the Indian Frontier was closed.

For more on the Indian Frontier, see page 11.

Now try this

Why do you think the American government felt threatened by the Ghost Dance movement? Write a short paragraph explaining your ideas.

Closing the Frontier

By 1890, the West was settled: railroads and towns covered what had previously been known as the Great American Desert. The Plains Indians had lost the struggle for the Plains and the Frontier was declared closed by the American government. This meant that the land that had once been Indian territory was now open to all.

For more on the Great American Desert, see page 1.

The resolution of 'the Indian Problem'

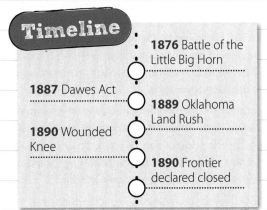

Timeline

1876 Battle of the Little Big Horn

1887 Dawes Act

1889 Oklahoma Land Rush

1890 Wounded Knee

1890 Frontier declared closed

The Oklahoma Land Rush

In April 1889, the American government offered 2 million acres of land, which had previously belonged to the Plains Indians, to white settlers. At noon a cannon was fired at a nearby fort and settlers simply had to race to stake a claim on a plot of land for it to become theirs. By evening all of the land had been claimed. A year later, the Frontier was closed and nearly all land became available.

The Battle of the Little Big Horn in 1876 hardened attitudes towards the Plains Indians and made white Americans and the American army determined to beat them.

For more on the Battle of the Little Big Horn, see pages 28–29.

The American government and the Plains Indians had made many treaties – such as the Fort Laramie Treaties and the Medicine Lodge Treaties – which included promises that were later broken by both sides.

The network of railroads that was built across the West transformed the Plains, bringing huge numbers of settlers to an area which had previously been thought of as unfit for settlement.

For more on railroads, see page 24.

Factors leading to the defeat of the Plains Indians

The reservation system destroyed the Plains Indians' way of life and the Dawes Act finally made it completely impossible for them to continue their traditional ways. Many Plains Indians didn't have the skills to live in an 'American' way and starvation and violence became widespread.

For more on the reservation system, see pages 11, 26 and 27. For more on the Dawes Act, see page 30.

The American government had many resources such as money and access to the latest technology for their army. The Plains Indians could not match these resources and often had weapons and communication systems that were inferior.

Cultural clashes and the concept of 'Manifest Destiny' meant that white Americans believed the Plains Indians were inferior. As a result, they feared the Plains Indians and felt that they should hand over the land they lived on and live like white Americans. In the later years of the conflict this often led to events like the massacres at Sand Creek and Wounded Knee, which show the strong feeling of many white Americans that Plains Indians should 'assimilate or die'. Some historians label these events as **genocide** (the deliberate killing of large groups of people from a particular ethnic group).

Although the Civil War meant the focus of the American army shifted away from harassing the Plains Indians, a number of Indian tribes chose to support the Confederate States. This made them very unpopular once the Union had won.

It's important to remember that life on the Plains was hard. The difficult conditions meant that everyone had to struggle to survive and attitudes towards others were harsh. As time went on, attitudes on both sides hardened.

Now try this

In a short paragraph, explain what you think was the most important reason for the defeat of the Plains Indians.

Exam overview

This page introduces you to the main features and requirements of the Paper 1 Section A exam paper for America, 1840–1895: Expansion and consolidation.

About Paper 1

- Paper 1 is for both your period study **and** your wider world depth study.

- Section A of the paper will be on your period study which is **America, 1840–1895: Expansion and consolidation.**

- You must answer all questions in Section A.

- You will receive two documents: a question paper, which will contain the questions and interpretations, and an answer booklet.

> The Paper 1 exam lasts for 1 hour 45 minutes (105 minutes). There are 84 marks in total: **40 marks for Section A**; 40 marks, plus 4 marks for spelling, punctuation and grammar, for Section B. You should spend approximately **50 minutes on Section A** and 50 minutes on Section B with 5 minutes to check your answers.

> Here we are focusing on Section A and your period study. However, the same exam papers will also include Section B, where you will answer questions about your wider world depth study.

The questions

The questions for Paper 1 Section A will always follow this pattern:

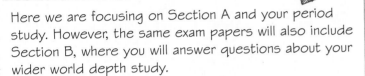

> You can see examples of all six questions on pages 36–41, and in the practice questions on pages 42–51.

Question 1

How does **Interpretation B** differ from **Interpretation A** about … ?

Explain your answer using **Interpretations A and B**.

(4 marks)

> Question 1 targets AO4. AO4 is about analysing, evaluating and making substantiated judgements. Spend about 5 minutes on this question, which is about **the ways in which the interpretations differ.**

Question 2

Why might the authors of **Interpretations A and B** have a different interpretation about …?

Explain your answer using **Interpretations A and B** and your contextual knowledge. **(4 marks)**

> Question 2 also targets AO4. Spend about 5 minutes on this question, which is about **suggesting and explaining why** the interpretations differ.

Question 3

Which interpretation do you find more convincing about …?

Explain your answer using **Interpretations A and B** and your contextual knowledge. **(8 marks)**

> Question 3 also targets AO4. You should spend approximately 10 minutes on this question, which is about **evaluating** the interpretations.

> Question 4 targets AO1. AO1 is about showing your knowledge and understanding of the **key features and characteristics** of the topic. Spend about 5 minutes on this question.

Question 4

Describe two … **(4 marks)**

Question 5

In what ways …?

Explain your answer. **(8 marks)**

> Question 5 targets both AO1 and AO2. AO2 is about explaining and analysing historical events using historical concepts, such as causation, consequence, change, continuity, similarity and difference. Spend about 10 minutes on this question, which focuses on **change: explaining how** a group or development was affected by something.

Question 6

Which of the following was the more important reason why …?

(Two bullet points)

Explain your answer with reference to both bullet points. **(12 marks)**

> Question 6 also targets both AO1 and AO2. Spend about 15 minutes on this question, which is about making a judgement and focuses on **causation, consequence, change and/or continuity.**

Interpretation skills

This exam asks you to analyse, evaluate and make judgements about interpretations.

What are interpretations?

For the first three questions in the exam paper you will be asked to study two different **interpretations** of a particular enquiry or event. Interpretations are compiled after the time period or event. Interpretations can be accounts of events written by people who were there or written later by historians. They might also be images, such as reconstructive drawings or diagrams of events. All interpretations will contain people's views and opinions.

As well as analysing interpretations, you will need to evaluate them and make judgements about them. In all cases, you need to keep the historical **context** in mind.

Analysing interpretations

When analysing interpretations you need to try to work out the **message** of the interpretation. Do this separately for each interpretation and then compare them. You then need to think about the following for the exam questions:

- **how** they differ (question 1)
- **why** they differ (question 2)
- which interpretation is **more convincing** (question 3).

Look at each interpretation carefully. Underline information or annotate the interpretation with your ideas to help you identify key points that you can use in your answer.

Contextual knowledge

Questions 2 and 3 will both ask you to explain your answer using the interpretations and your **contextual knowledge**. This means that you need to think about what you know about the event or development and how the interpretations fit with what you know. Only use knowledge that's relevant to the topic in the question and that is linked to what is discussed in the interpretation itself.

As you consider each interpretation, ask yourself: What do I know about these events/developments? How is this reflected in the interpretation? How is this linked to the focus of the question?

Provenance

Before both interpretations in the exam paper you will be given several lines of **provenance**. This will vary for each but is likely to include some details about the author and their work or experiences, and when their work was published. This information is as important as the interpretation itself as it will help you establish the **purpose** of the interpretation, which will help you in questions 2 and 3 in particular.

Provenance means where something comes from – where it started or came into existence.

Hints and tips for analysing and evaluating interpretations

How complete?	How objective?	What is the chosen emphasis?
The interpretations can be different because they are concerned with finding out about different aspects of the enquiry and may cover different ground. Sometimes, historians set out to look at one aspect specifically, whereas others may want to look at related issues in a broader sense.	Historians can hold different views because they come from a particular school of thought. Therefore, their questions and answers are shaped by their wider views of society and how it works and has worked in the past. This can have an important impact on the judgements and opinions they hold about historical matters.	Sometimes, historians use the same sources but reach different views because they place a different level of importance on the same evidence. They may have access to the same material sources as each other, but will draw different conclusions about the significance of that evidence.

Interpretations A and B

These interpretations are referred to in the worked examples on pages 36–38.

SECTION A

America, 1840–1895: Expansion and consolidation

Read **Interpretations A** and **B** and answer questions 1, 2 and 3 on pages 36, 37 and 38.

Interpretation A   An article by David Keys, a journalist specialising in archaeology, about a ten-year archaeological and historical investigation into the Battle of the Little Big Horn led by an archaeologist called Dr Richard Allen Fox. The article was published in the *Independent* newspaper, 14 August 1993.

For each interpretation, underline or highlight any important words or phrases and annotate them.

> Custer's men were picked off by Indian riflemen as they attempted to hide behind the carcasses of their dead horses. There was probably no hand-to-hand fighting, and definitely no glorious last stand…
>
> It had long been thought that Custer was intent on attacking the village itself. Now it appears that he had headed off in pursuit of its inhabitants. His task at the time was to force the Indian population back into a reservation.
>
> Dr Fox's archaeological work has shed considerable new light on why Custer lost the battle. Custer's decision to disperse[1] his 210-strong force to four separate locations spread over 250 acres of terrain appears to have been a major tactical error.

[1]**disperse**: split up or separate

Your annotations on the interpretation could also include any points that contrast with the other interpretation.

Interpretation B   Lakota Chief Red Horse gave an eyewitness account of the Battle of the Little Big Horn, recorded in writing at the Cheyenne River Reservation in 1881. Chief Red Horse was a warrior of the Lakota Sioux who fought at the Battle of the Little Big Horn.

For each interpretation you will be given short details on the work the interpretation comes from. In this case, the eyewitness and when the account was written down.

You will be given a few lines of information about the author and/or the interpretation. In this case, you are told that the account was given by a warrior of the Lakota Sioux who took part in the Battle of the Little Big Horn.

> I soon saw that the soldiers were charging the camp… Among the soldiers was an officer who rode a horse with four white feet… the Sioux say this officer was the bravest man they had ever fought. I don't know whether this was Gen. Custer or not. ... The soldiers set fire to the lodges… Had the soldiers not divided I think they would have killed many Sioux. The different soldiers [i.e. Custer's battalion] that the Sioux killed made five brave stands[1]…The soldiers killed 136 and wounded 160 Sioux. The Sioux killed all these different soldiers in the ravine.

[1]**brave stands**: displays of great courage

It's a good idea to compare and contrast the provenance of the two interpretations. Why might they have a different view? Are they looking at different things? At different times? In different ways?

Question 1: Explaining how interpretations differ

Question 1 on your exam paper will ask you to identify differences in two interpretations: 'What is the main difference between the views...'. There are 4 marks available for this question.

Worked example

Read Interpretations A and B on page 35.

How does **Interpretation B** differ from **Interpretation A** about the details of the Battle of the Little Big Horn?

Explain your answer, using **Interpretations A** and **B**.

(4 marks)

Remember to include points from **both** interpretations. It's important to refer directly to the interpretation and include short quotations to support what you say.

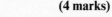 **Links**   You can revise the Battle of the Little Big Horn on pages 28 and 29.

How interpretations differ

In a question that asks **how** one interpretation differs from another, you need to analyse both interpretations and explain how they are different. Look for the important or key differences, not just surface details. A fundamental difference might be that they believe different factors are more important for explaining why something happened. A surface detail would just repeat content from the interpretations without explaining how they are different. You don't need to explain why they are different, as you will do this in question 2.

Sample answer

These interpretations are different because the first one says that there was no glorious last stand, whereas Chief Red Horse's account suggests that the American soldiers fought bravely.

 This answer focuses on one simple difference in surface detail instead of showing key, underlying differences in the interpretations.

Improved answer

Use short quotations to support your analysis.

In Interpretation A the journalist writing the piece claims that Custer did not attack the village, but 'headed off in pursuit of its inhabitants'. He argues that there was 'no glorious last stand' and that Custer's men were killed while trying to hide 'behind the carcasses of their dead horses'. The journalist gives the impression that Custer's mistake led to his men being slaughtered.

Make sure you focus on the **key points of difference**. Here the student does this well by discussing the fact that Interpretation A claims that Custer made mistakes and soldiers were killed while trying to hide, whereas Interpretation B claims Custer was brave and that his men fought courageously.

This is significantly different from Interpretation B in which Chief Red Horse claims that the soldiers 'were charging the camp'. He suggests that a man that was possibly Custer was 'the bravest man' the Sioux had ever fought. Red Horse also claims that Custer's soldiers made 'five brave stands', and that they 'killed 136' Sioux and 'wounded 160' more before they were defeated.

 You need to support your discussion with detailed points from **both** interpretations.

Think about the language you use in your answer, such as: 'argues', 'giving the impression', 'claims', and 'is significantly different'. These phrases help you to create a better answer because they show you are **analysing** another person's judgement or opinion about something.

Question 2: Explaining why interpretations differ

Question 2 on your exam paper will ask you to explain why two interpretations give different views. There are 4 marks available for this question.

Worked example

Why might **Interpretations A** and **B** on page 35 show a different understanding of the details of the Battle of the Little Big Horn?

Explain your answer using **Interpretations A** and **B** and your contextual knowledge. **(4 marks)**

Remember: you **must** include contextual knowledge in your answer.

'Why' questions

In a question that asks you why interpretations have different views, you need to offer and explain an idea about **why** there are differences. You need to show you understand that historical interpretations are judgements and opinions based on evidence and that, as such, different views can exist.

 Links You can revise the Battle of the Little Big Horn on pages 28 and 29.

Sample answer

Interpretations A and B might show a different understanding because they are each speaking to a different audience. Also, Chief Red Horse was at the Battle of the Little Big Horn, but the author of Interpretation A was not.

This answer makes two very good points but needs to develop them further by explaining **how this might affect** the interpretations.

Improved answer

Interpretations A and B might have a different understanding because they use different sources of information. The journalist in Interpretation A is writing about the conclusions of an archaeological and historical investigation. However, these conclusions could be inaccurate as they are drawn from what was left behind after the battle, and cannot say exactly what happened at the time. The journalist is also writing for a modern audience, who might not think that Custer was a war hero as many people did at the time.

In Interpretation B, Chief Red Horse was actually at the battle, and is working from memory. However, he is speaking five years later and his memory might be wrong. He might also want to support the idea that Custer was a hero so that the public might think better of the Plains Indians who – by the time this account was recorded – were suffering badly on small reservations, partly because of public pressure after the Battle of the Little Big Horn. This shows that the interpretations might be different because of the audiences that they were produced for.

This answer makes two good points and goes on to explain **how this might affect their interpretation**. This helps to make the answer a strong one.

You should always read the **provenance** of the interpretations carefully as this student obviously has. It will give you important clues about the focus of the interpretations and the evidence used.

Make sure you include your own **contextual knowledge**. This student has taken a number of opportunities to show their knowledge of the event.

You must refer to **both** interpretations as this student has done.

Question 3: Evaluating interpretations

Question 3 on your exam paper will ask you to evaluate two interpretations by asking which interpretation you find more convincing. There are 8 marks available for this question.

Worked example

Which interpretation do you find more convincing about the details of the Battle of the Little Big Horn?

Explain your answer using **Interpretations A** and **B** on page 35 and your contextual knowledge. **(8 marks)**

Which is more convincing?

You must:
- ☑ explore different views on the debate
- ☑ reach a clear **judgement** yourself
- ☑ give detailed knowledge of the **context** and wider issues
- ☑ use **both** interpretations – don't just rely on one.

Links You can revise the Battle of the Little Big Horn on pages 28 and 29.

Sample extract

I find Interpretation B more convincing as Chief Red Horse was actually at the Battle of the Little Big Horn. The interpretation says that the Plains Indians did not start the battle and that the soldiers attacked the camp, which happened at a time when exterminators wanted to get rid of the Plains Indians and other people wanted to push them back onto their reservations. Chief Red Horse also admits that the Sioux killed all of the soldiers so he is obviously telling the truth.

Remember: you **must** include your own contextual knowledge in your answer.

Get straight to the answer and give your opinion clearly, as this student has done.

Support the points you make with **evidence** from the interpretation and **your own knowledge**. This student picks out information from the interpretation that supports their contextual knowledge but also needs to look at which elements do not fit with their knowledge.

You **must** refer to **both** interpretations in your answer – the student doesn't do this here.

Improved extract

The claims made in Interpretation A about there being 'no glorious last stand' at the Battle of the Little Big Horn are based on historical and archaeological evidence. They seem to be backed up by other accounts given at the time about how the battle was over within an hour, so Interpretation A is more convincing about this point.

While Red Horse says in Interpretation B that Custer was brave, his account agrees with Interpretation A when he says that Custer made a 'major tactical error' in splitting his troops: 'Had the soldiers not divided I think they would have killed many Sioux'.

Chief Red Horse seems to have no reason to lie about Custer's tactics in 'charging the camp' and having the soldiers 'set fire to the lodges'. Custer had attacked women and children in villages before, and may not have wanted to just 'force the Indian population back into a reservation' as argued in Interpretation A. Interpretation B is more convincing about this element.

You could highlight key points in the interpretations themselves to help you focus on the arguments that you need to evaluate in order to make your judgement.

Make sure you engage directly with **both** interpretations and challenge both of them, as this student does.

Use short quotations to illustrate your points, as this student does.

You need to put both interpretations into **context** as the student has done here by bringing in their own knowledge of the events leading up to the battle as well as the battle itself.

Question 4: Describing features or characteristics

Question 4 on your exam paper will ask you to describe two features or characteristics of America, 1840–1895. There are 4 marks available for this question.

Worked example

Describe two difficulties that the Plains Indians faced after the Dawes Act of 1887.   **(4 marks)**

 **Links** For more on the Dawes Act, see page 30.

 You may be asked to identify two of the following: issues, difficulties, features, problems or solutions.

 To answer this question you need to identify **two** difficulties and show some understanding of **each** one.

What does 'describe' mean?

Describe means give an account of the main characteristics of something. You should develop your description with relevant details to show that you understand them. However, you do not need to include reasons or justifications.

Sample answer

After the Battle of the Little Big Horn the American public wanted the Plains Indians off the reservations and to force them to live like white people. After the Dawes Act the Plains Indians had to farm like white people but it did not work and many of them starved. Also they were expected to give up their traditional ways of life. They had to live in much smaller family units and their children were sent to boarding schools. Some Plains Indians became American citizens instead of being tribal members.

 Read the question carefully. This question asks for difficulties faced by the Plains Indians after the Dawes Act, so the information about public opinion after the Little Big Horn is irrelevant.

 Make sure you only give **two** difficulties and that you describe each one with some detail. This answer lists more than two difficulties and does not give any detail.

Improved answer

After the Dawes Act the Plains Indians were expected to farm like white people. Although the government set up training programmes to teach the Plains Indians about agriculture, they were not suited to farming. They had been brought up as warriors and the land they were given was not good enough to farm and support their families. Consequently, many Indian families starved or had their land taken away from them and given to white settlers.

In addition, Plains Indians who accepted the government's offer of land became American citizens instead of being tribal members. This meant they were unable to maintain their traditional identities and had to stick to American law just like everyone else, which did not allow for some of the traditional Indian customs. It also meant that Plains Indians who did not take up the government offer were not citizens and were considered to be outlaws who were hunted and jailed, or even killed.

 It's a good idea to separate your two difficulties in different paragraphs as the student has done here. This shows clearly that you have identified two separate difficulties.

 Using words like 'consequently' shows that you are giving supporting detail.

 This answer gives good **supporting detail** for **both** difficulties. There is more that could be said about each problem but don't forget this question is only worth 4 marks.

Question 5: Explaining change

Question 5 on your exam paper will ask you to explain how a group or development was affected by something. There are 8 marks available for this question.

Worked example

In what ways were the lives of the Mormons affected by persecution?

Explain your answer. **(8 marks)**

Sample extract

Wherever the Mormons went there was a lot of anti-Mormon feeling, which meant that they had to move frequently. They regularly faced violence. The violent persecution of Mormons became so bad that in 1844 Smith was murdered, meaning they had to find a new leader.

A key reason behind the anti-Mormon feeling was the Mormons' practice of polygamy. Because many Americans disliked the practice, the Mormons faced violence in many of the places they settled in and so they looked outside America for places to move to, such as the Salt Lake Valley.

Persecution did affect the lives of the Mormons in more positive ways by driving them to make a success of things though. For example, Brigham Young and others saw the move to the Salt Lake Valley as a chance to get away from persecution for good, and this made them organise the move carefully. Also, once they were there, Young knew he couldn't rely on outsiders to supply what they needed, partly because of the persecution they had suffered. He therefore set about finding solutions to different problems to carefully ensure they could lead a successful and prosperous life.

Explaining 'in what ways'

This question requires you to identify and explain how and why a group or development was affected by something – how it **changed**. There will always be a number of different ways in which change happened. The best answers will also show that change was not the same for everyone or everything.

Links You can revise the Mormons on pages 3, 4 and 20.

Give an example of **change**: this answer gives the example of how the Mormons faced violence. Support your example with **details**: this student gives the details of a number of instances of violence and goes on to say what effect this had.

Try to explain the **reasons** for the changes that took place. In this case, the student points out that the practice of polygamy caused a good deal of persecution, making it difficult for Mormons to come to terms with other Americans and causing them to leave America.

Using the question wording in your answer makes it clear you are staying focused on the question.

The best answers will show that not everyone's lives were affected in the same way. Here, the student talks about how Brigham Young made the move to the Salt Lake Valley a success as a result of his desire to lead the Mormons away from persecution for good.

Question 6: Making a judgement

Question 6 on your exam paper will identify two reasons for you and ask you to analyse them. You will need to decide which was the more important reason why something did or did not happen. There are 12 marks available for this question.

Worked example

Which of the following was the more important reason for the continued settlement of the American West after the Civil War:

- railroads
- American government policy?

Explain your answer with reference to both bullet points.   **(12 marks)**

Sample extract

Both the railroads and American government policy were important reasons for the continued settlement of the West after the Civil War.

The railroads were important for a number of reasons. Firstly, they allowed people to travel west much more quickly. Secondly they allowed people to go west to claim their homesteads and to send produce back to the East to sell. In addition, the railroads ran big marketing campaigns aimed at encouraging people to move to the West from the East, the South and also from Europe, where people wanted to escape poor conditions and religious persecution.

Government policy was also important, and was closely linked to the development of the railroads. The government passed laws which allowed the railroad companies to build. The government also encouraged the railroad companies to attract people to the West. For example, the government gave the railroad companies the land for two miles either side of the new railroads to give to people to settle on. This was an important reason in the settlement of the West after the Civil War as a number of people, including freed slaves from the South, were looking for a new, prosperous way of life.

The balance of Assessment Objectives

Question 6 is an essay question, which is worth 12 marks in total. Of this, 6 marks are for AO1 and 6 marks are for AO2. Therefore you need to combine information and understanding (AO1) equally with analysis and explanation (AO2) for the best results. You also need to reach a judgement and follow a sustained line of reasoning which is coherent, relevant, substantiated and logically structured.

Links For more on the continued settlement of the American West after the Civil War, see page 24.

Begin your answer with a strong opening statement. This should lay out **your opinion** of the reasons given in the question and their importance.

You **must** explain **both** reasons given in the bullet points, giving details of what happened and why.

Only focus on the reasons given in the bullet points in the question, as the student has done here. **You don't need to include any other reasons in your answer.**

Make sure you show how the reasons are **connected**. Here, the student points out that government policy was important for the development of the railroads.

In a full answer, make sure you demonstrate a **sustained line of reasoning** and that you reach a **judgement** about which reason was more important.

This is an extract from a student's answer. In a full answer, you could go on to discuss other ways in which these reasons encouraged settlement in the West after the Civil War – for example, other things the government did such as the renewed promotion of 'Manifest Destiny' and moving the Plains Indians onto the reservations.

Practice

You will need to refer to the interpretations below in your answers to questions 1, 2 and 3 on pages 43–45.

SECTION A

America, 1840–1895: Expansion and consolidation

Answer **all six questions** on pages 43 to 50.

Read **Interpretations A** and **B** and answer questions **1**, **2** and **3** on pages 43–45.

Interpretation A   Dr James McPherson writing for the website of the American Battlefield Trust. McPherson is an American Civil War historian writing in the present day. The American Battlefield Trust is a charity focused on the preservation of battlefields in the United States, including those from the Civil War.

> The Civil War started because of uncompromising differences between the free and slave states over the power of the national government to prohibit slavery .... When Abraham Lincoln won election in 1860 as the first Republican president ... pledging to keep slavery out of the territories, seven slave states in the deep South seceded and formed a new nation, the Confederate States of America. ... Most of the Northern people refused to recognize the legitimacy of secession. They feared that it would discredit democracy and create a fatal precedent[1] that would eventually fragment the no-longer United States into several small, squabbling countries.

[1] **precedent:** an earlier event or action that is seen as an example to follow.

Interpretation B   W.E.B. Du Bois in his book *Black Reconstruction in America*, published in 1935. Du Bois was the first African American to earn a doctorate, in 1895. He was a sociologist (someone who studies society), historian, and civil rights activist.

> Easily the most dramatic episode in American history was the sudden move to free four million black slaves in an effort to stop a great civil war, to end forty years of bitter controversy, and to appease[1] the moral sense of civilization.
>
> From the day of its birth, the anomaly[2] of slavery plagued a nation which asserted the equality of all men, and sought to derive[3] powers of government from the consent of the governed. Within sound of the voices of those who said this lived more than half a million black slaves, forming nearly one-fifth of the population of a new nation.

[1] **appease:** make someone less angry or hostile
[2] **anomaly:** something inconsistent or that doesn't fit
[3] **derive:** obtain

Practice

Put your skills and knowledge into practice with the following question. You will need to refer to Interpretations A and B on page 42 in your answer.

1 How does **Interpretation B** differ from **Interpretation A** about the causes of the American Civil War?

Explain your answer, using **Interpretations A** and **B**.

(4 marks)

Guided   Interpretations A and B both discuss the causes
of the Civil War, but offer different views.

....

....

....

....

....

....

....

....

....

....

....

....

....

....

....

....

....

....

....

You have 1 hour 45 minutes for the **whole** of Paper 1, which means you have **50 minutes** for **Section A**. You should use the time carefully to answer all the questions fully. In the exam, leave 5 minutes or so to check your work when you've finished both Sections A and B.

Links You can revise the causes of the Civil War on pages 16–18.

You can revise how to evaluate interpretations on page 34.

Spend about **5 minutes** on this answer. You must identify the **key points of difference**, rather than just surface differences.

Make sure you refer to detail in **both** interpretations.

Remember to use specific words and phrases in your answer such as: 'argues', 'claims', 'states' and 'backs this up'. These help show you are analysing another person's judgement or opinion.

It's a good idea to use **short quotations** from the interpretations to support your answer.

Remember: you don't need to explain **why** the interpretations are different.

43

Practice

Put your skills and knowledge into practice with the following question. You will need to refer to Interpretations A and B on page 42 in your answer.

---

2 Why might the authors of **Interpretations** **A** and **B** have a different interpretation about the causes of the American Civil War?

Explain your answer using **Interpretations** **A** and **B** and your contextual knowledge. **(4 marks)**

(Guided) Interpretations A and B might have different

interpretations about the causes of the American Civil War

because ....

....

....

....

....

....

....

....

....

....

....

....

....

....

....

....

....

....

....

You should spend about **5 minutes** on this answer.

 Links You can revise the causes of the Civil War on pages 16–18.

You can revise how to evaluate interpretations on page 34.

Remember that the **provenance** information given before each interpretation will help you with this question.

It is important to use your own **contextual knowledge** in answering this question.

A good way of answering this specific question is to think about the focus of each author. McPherson's focus is on the wider politics of the Civil War era, whereas W.E.B. Du Bois is discussing how slavery contradicted American values.

Make sure you refer to **both** the interpretations to support your answer.

Practice

Put your skills and knowledge into practice with the following question. You will need to refer to Interpretations A and B on page 42 in your answer.

You should spend about 10 minutes on this question.

3 Which interpretation do you find more convincing about the causes of the American Civil War?

Explain your answer using **Interpretations A** and **B** and your contextual knowledge. **(8 marks)**

 Links You can revise the causes of the Civil War on pages 16–18.

Guided I find Interpretation _____ more convincing because _____

....

Start with a clear **judgement** stating which interpretation you think is more convincing.

....

....

....

....

You can revise how to evaluate interpretations on page 34.

....

....

....

You could include reasons why the other interpretation is less convincing at this early stage.

....

....

....

....

....

It's essential to refer to **both** interpretations throughout your answer.

....

....

....

....

Remember to include your own knowledge of the **context** – about the causes of disagreement and struggles for power in the years leading up to the Civil War.

....

....

....

....

It doesn't really matter which interpretation you find more convincing. There isn't a 'correct' answer as you are asked for your own opinion. What's important is to explain **why** you think that particular interpretation is more convincing and give supporting **evidence** from your contextual knowledge.

....

....

....

....

Practice

Use this page to continue your answer to question 3.

....

....

....

....

....

....

....

....

....

....

....

....

....

← You should build an argument throughout your answer, giving a number of reasons why one interpretation is more convincing and the other one less convincing.

← The best answers should look at how each interpretation fits with your knowledge, and how it does not. There may be elements of truth in both interpretations. In this case, both agree that slavery was a major contributing factor to the Civil War, even if they do not agree on why that was.

Practice

Put your skills and knowledge into practice with the following question.

4 Describe two problems faced by migrants travelling west in the 1840s.　　　**(4 marks)**

....

....

....

....

....

....

....

....

....

....

....

....

....

....

....

....

....

....

....

You should spend about **5 minutes** on this question.

Links You can revise the problems faced by migrants in the 1840s on page 6.

Only describe **two** problems. You won't receive any credit for describing more than two and will waste valuable time if you do.

Write a separate paragraph for each of your two problems. This will show you have identified two different problems.

You need to include some **details** for each problem. This will show that you understand **how** it was a problem.

Problems could include: lack of supplies; conditions on the Great Plains; disease.

Practice

Put your skills and knowledge into practice with the following question.

5 In what ways were the lives of Americans affected by the California Gold Rush?

Explain your answer.   **(8 marks)**

Guided The lives of Americans were affected by the

California Gold Rush because ....

....

....

....

....

....

....

....

....

....

....

....

....

....

....

....

....

....

....

....

....

....

....

....

....

You should spend about 10 minutes on this question.

Links You can revise the California Gold Rush on page 7.

You need to identify the **changes** in people's lives. Remember to include a number of **different ways** in which people's lives were affected.

Each example of change you describe must be supported with **detail**.

Don't forget you can include both positive and negative changes in your answer. For example, in this case, California became more developed and prosperous, but tensions with the Plains Indians were made worse.

Practice

Use this page to continue your answer to question 5.

....

....

....

....

....

....

....

....

....

....

....

....

◀ For each change you describe, try to explain the **reason** why this change happened. For example, the Gold Rush helped the economy because California's economy grew very strong very quickly.

Practice

Put your skills and knowledge into practice with the following question.

6 Which of the following was the more important reason for the decline in Plains Indian culture after 1865:

- the Dawes Act
- the closing of the Frontier?

Explain your answer with reference to both bullet points.

(12 marks)

You should spend about 15 minutes on this question.

Links You can revise the causes of the decline of Plains Indian culture on pages 30–32.

Guided The Dawes Act and the closing of the Frontier were both important reasons behind the decline of Plains Indian culture. However, I think the more important reason was

In your opening paragraph, come to a **judgement** about which reason was more important.

....

....

....

....

Remember that you need to concentrate equally on giving information to show what you know about the events in the bullet points **and** analysing and explaining how they led to the decline of Plains Indian culture.

....

....

....

....

....

....

....

....

Examine **both** of the bullet points given in the question and give detailed information on both of them throughout your answer.

....

....

....

....

....

You don't need to include any other reasons besides the ones given in the bullet points. You just need to **evaluate** the two given reasons.

....

....

Practice

Use this page to continue your answer to question 6.

....
....
....
....
....
....
....
....
....
....
....
....
....
....
....
....
....
....
....
....
....
....
....
....
....
....

⬅ If possible, you should also show how the two reasons given in the bullet points are **connected** to each other. For example, the Dawes Act and the closing of the Frontier were both caused by the American government's determination to make the Plains Indians fit in with their way of life.

⬅ Try to build a line of argument throughout the whole essay.

ANSWERS

Where an exemplar answer is given, this is not necessarily the only correct response. In most cases there is a range of responses that can gain full marks.

SUBJECT CONTENT

Expansion: opportunities and challenges

1. The Great American Desert

The main reason that people thought the Great Plains were uninhabitable was reports by explorers like Stephen Long, who described the plains as 'The Great American Desert'. The lack of trees meant a shortage of wood to build houses, and there was very little natural water. The flat landscape meant that there was no protection from strong winds – hot in summer and bitterly cold in winter. The presence of wolves and locusts was another barrier to farming the land.

2. 'Manifest Destiny'

'Manifest Destiny' involved the idea that God wanted white settlers to go west. The painting shows this by having an image of a woman who looks like an angel, a messenger from God, who is leading the white American settlers west.

3. The Mormons: persecution

Religious, any two from:
- People were against the practice of polygamy.
- The Mormons claimed to be Christian but were unlike other Christian groups.
- The speed with which the movement grew and moved into existing communities worried people.

Economic, any two from:
- The Mormons encouraged freedom for slaves which would have a big economic impact.
- The financial crash made people angry and they wanted someone to blame. As Joseph Smith had a bank that collapsed in the crash he was a good target.
- People thought that Joseph Smith was planning to overthrow the government and impose his beliefs, leading to further economic disruption.

4. The Mormons: Great Salt Lake

The Mormons faced the problem that they did not know what they would find when they arrived at the Great Salt Lake. Brigham Young spoke to several guides (including Plains Indians) to find out as much as possible about the site before they got there. This meant they were able to prepare in advance.

5. Journey west: push and pull

Push, any one from:
- The financial crisis left a lot of people out of work so they thought they would have better prospects in the West.
- Persecuted groups, such as the Mormons, sought freedom in the West.
- There was a shortage of suitable farming land in the East/ overpopulation made worse by the expansion of the cities.

Pull, any one from:
- The government and newspapers promoted the idea of 'Manifest Destiny' so many white settlers thought it was their God-given responsibility to populate the whole of America. This led them to go west out of a sense of duty.
- Positive stories from people who had gone west before, such as fur trappers, led to people following them.
- The government offered free land which people could not have afforded in the East.

6. Journey west: pioneer trails

We took a shortcut that ended up adding a lot of time to our journey, and went over difficult land. The wagons and animals often got stuck or damaged and we had to walk a lot. Because the route was difficult and took much longer than we'd expected, we ran out of food. Everyone was arguing with each other, and someone was even killed. Lots of the animals starved, and when we got stuck over the winter, people started starving too. When people died, we had no choice but to eat their bodies, desperate to stay alive until we were rescued.

7. The miners

The Gold Rush caused problems because of increased traffic which crossed Indian territory and sacred lands. The migrants had a different view of how the land should be treated compared to the Plains Indians and the impact that they had on rivers and wildlife made life harder for the Plains Indians to survive. The Gold Rush also caused problems for the Californian Indians as tensions with migrants led to widespread violence.

8. Plains Indians: way of life

The Plains Indians relied on buffalo to supply all their needs (meat, leather, fur, bone, horn). Horses were vital to provide transport for the Plains Indians who were nomadic and followed the buffalo herds as they migrated. Hunting on horseback was more efficient than hunting on foot, making it easier for the Indians to live. Horses also made it easier for the nomadic Plains Indians to move and carry their belongings.

9. Plains Indians: beliefs

For example, three from:
- The Plains Indians did not believe that the land could be owned but the white settlers, encouraged by 'Manifest Destiny', came west with exactly that purpose.
- Most of the white settlers were Christian and the Plains Indians' ideas about spirits and the spirit world offended them.
- Dances like the war dance were very intimidating and frightening for the white settlers.
- The Plains Indians believed that farming was disrespectful to the land, and the settlers were settling in order to farm.

10. Plains Indians: tribes and warfare

Any two from:
- The Plains Indians were governed by group discussion and agreement. The white Americans thought that laws should be created by the government and they should be obeyed.
- White settlers did not understand that a chief could not force his people to obey him since he had no power over them.
- White settlers thought that laws were important to keep order. However, the Indians did not have any laws as they knew that their tribe would not survive unless everyone behaved well.

11. The Permanent Indian Frontier

The American government and the white people of America believed that the Great Plains were impossible to settle on. As a result, they handed them over to the Plains Indians and put in place a Permanent Indian Frontier with forts along it. The idea was that the Indians could live on the worthless land beyond the Frontier without American government interference.

12. Changing relationships

Relationships between the white settlers and Plains Indians changed because the amount of contact between them changed. At first, the Plains Indians saw white migrants simply passing by on their way to other places, but then they started settling on land that the Indians lived on. This meant the two groups had much more contact and white settlers developed prejudices against the Plains Indians as they witnessed more of their different lifestyle.

Conflict across America

13. Fort Laramie Treaty, 1851

Any three from:
- The failure of the policy of concentration.
- The Indians and the American government had an official relationship in a way they had not before.
- Compensation for tribes who stuck to the Treaty, which was not always paid.
- Migrants were only supposed to cross Indian land but in reality they often settled on it.
- The government failed to protect the Plains tribes from white Americans, and stop them from settling in Indian territory as they'd agreed.

14. Indian Wars, 1862–1867: 1

For example, five from:
- White settlers thought that they were better than the Plains Indians, and entitled to their own land for farming.
- A clash of cultures meant that white settlers and the American government did not understand the Indian way of life, and were afraid of them.
- Poor conditions on reservations meant that many tribes were starving, and struggling to survive. Conflict with local traders meant that they could not even buy food.
- Because they did not have elected officials, their chiefs could not speak for all of them or agree to treaties that everyone would obey. Many Plains Indians were angry about the treaties, and continued to hunt and act as they had before.
- The American government broke the treaties, failing to make promised payments and allowing white settlers to move into Indian lands.
- The discovery of gold and the need for more land meant that tribes were moved onto much smaller areas of land that were more difficult to survive on.

15. Indian Wars, 1862–1867: 2

For the **Sand Creek Massacre**, any two from:
- More than 150 Cheyenne were killed.
- Some Plains Indians escaped to tell others that they were killed while surrendering, and mistrust of white Americans grew.
- The death of the Indian chiefs who wanted peace with white Americans led to a more hostile approach.

For **Fetterman's Trap**, any two from:
- 81 American soldiers were killed.
- The American government agreed to abandon the Bozeman Trail and three forts.
- Red Cloud agreed to move his people to a much smaller reservation.

16. North vs South

Any three from:
- The federal nature of American government led to power struggles between states and the government.
- There were major social and cultural differences between the North and the South.
- Free states started calling for slavery to be banned but slave states did not agree and threatened to leave the Union.
- The westward expansion of America meant that tension over slavery grew as the federal American government tried to restrict slavery in new territories.
- Slavery was hugely important to the economy of the agricultural South where the majority of slaves worked on plantations.

17. Growing tensions

The poster suggests that the book *Uncle Tom's Cabin* was very popular and influential saying it is the 'the greatest book of the age' and that 270 000 copies have been sold, which shows the impact it had on popular opinion. The novel was written to promote the abolition of slavery, which became an even more popular idea in the North after the novel came out. Slavery was a very controversial topic and caused some Southern states to decide to leave the Union, which in turn led to the Civil War.

18. Outbreak of war

For example:
Long-term causes:
- Economic differences between North and South
- The American Revolutionary War (1775–1783)
- Tensions between federal government and the states
Medium-term causes:
- Missouri Compromise (1820)
- Kansas–Nebraska Act (1854)
- Nat Turner's Rebellion (1831)
Short-term causes:
- Election of Lincoln (1860)
- Secession of South Carolina (1860)
- Battle of Fort Sumter (1861).

19. Impacts of the war

Thanks to the invention of the telegraph news could reach people faster than ever before. As a result, people far away from the battle locations were able to receive news and details of the war. For the first time graphic photos of battles, like Gettysburg, were included in newspapers so people had a clearer picture of what was happening. This information was sent out quickly after it happened in a way the American public had never experienced before.

20. Mountain Meadows Massacre, 1857

The cartoon is meant to warn migrants about the dangers of the Mormons in Utah. It shows a group of women and children lining up to walk into the mouth of a skull labelled 'Utah'. It shows that many Americans were afraid that migrants might be lured to the state with promises, and then harmed (or even killed) in the same way that they were at the Mountain Meadows Massacre. It is also possible the cartoonist was afraid women would be drawn into polygamy by the Mormon men shown in the eyes of the skull.

Consolidation: forging the nation

21. Reunifying the nation

The picture shows that despite passing federal laws to protect African Americans, groups like the Ku Klux Klan were still taking violent action against them. This shows that the Civil Rights Act of 1866 was not very effective and why the Civil Rights Act of 1870 had to be passed to make it clear that it was a federal offence to attack or threaten African Americans.

22. Reconstruction in the South

During Presidential Reconstruction, Southern states were allowed to govern themselves as long as they did not allow slavery and paid off their war debts. However, under Radical Reconstruction, the South was placed under military rule and had to agree to certain things if they wanted to rejoin the Union.

23. Freed slaves

Changed, any two from:
- Many freed slaves worked for wages on plantations, but failed harvests meant they did not get paid.
- Freed slaves eventually got the vote.
- Black Americans were elected to government.

Stayed the same, any two from:
- White Southerners' attitudes to freed slaves were the same as before so many didn't pay their black employees.
- Violence against former slaves was common.
- Black Americans continued to have their rights restricted by Black Codes.

24. Reasons for going west

The building of the railroads and the promotions offered by the railroad companies were major pull factors for migrants after the Civil War. The railroads meant that people were able to move to the West quickly and cheaply, and to send their farm produce back to the East for sale once they got there. The railroad companies offered financial incentives to move west, such as free land and discounted travel.

25. Homesteaders

(This example focuses on small land holdings. Other answers could also consider settlers' isolation or the railroads.)
The Homestead Act allowed people to claim 160 acres of land, but this was not really enough to support a family. To help them, the government passed the Timber Culture Act of 1873, which let people get another 160 acres so long as they planted trees on half of that land. The Desert Land Act of 1877 then let them buy 640 acres of desert for very little money. They could then try to improve that land so that it was more suitable for growing crops and grazing their animals.

26. Small reservations policy

By 1865 the Plains Indians were seen as a big threat to the development of the West that white Americans wanted. Railroad companies wanted to build on their land and much larger numbers of white settlers were coming to the Plains and these people felt threatened by the Plains Indians. To make room for the new settlers and the planned development, the American government had to break up the huge Indian reservation. Instead several smaller reservations were created, which also meant that a large proportion of the land was taken away from the Plains Indians completely.

27. Attitudes and adaptations

Exterminators, one from:
- Indian Appropriations Act
- Wiping out the buffalo

Humanitarians, one from:
- Boarding schools for Indian children to teach them to assimilate
- Moving Plains Indians onto reservations.

28. Little Big Horn: growing tensions and battle

Tensions had been high in the area as the Plains Indians were unhappy with the policy of moving them onto reservations. When gold was discovered in the Lakota Sioux hunting lands, gold prospectors ignored the 1868 Fort Laramie Treaty and set up camp in the area. This upset the Plains Indians even more. The American government failed to buy the land from the Sioux and then accused them of breaking the Treaty themselves. The government then threatened the Sioux with attack.

29. Little Big Horn: responsibilities and consequences

Different answers are possible as long as you give reasons for your views. For example:
Custer was mainly to blame for the defeat of the 7th Cavalry at the Little Big Horn as he tired his men and horses out on a difficult journey through the Wolf Mountains rather than going around them as instructed. He also ignored the orders to make camp and wait for reinforcements and chose instead to attack the Plains Indians with too few men.

30. The Dawes Act, 1887

Any two from:
- The Dawes Act divided up the reservations into individual farms, splitting up the tribes.
- Boarding schools were set up to teach Indian children to be more 'American'.
- Indian tribal status was removed – all Plains Indians were now Americans. However, only those who cooperated with the government were allowed to become citizens.

31. Wounded Knee, 1890

The American people had been shocked by the defeat at the Little Big Horn and saw the Plains Indians as a threat. With the Dawes Act, they had tried to control the Plains Indians and stamp out their culture. The Ghost Dance movement showed that the traditional beliefs were still alive, and that the Plains Indians were prepared to resist. Also, white Americans often found the Indian sacred dances strange and frightening.

32. Closing the Frontier

Different answers are possible as long as you give reasons for your choice. For example:
The reservation system was the most important reason for the defeat of the Plains Indians because they could not adapt to life on the small reservations. Here, they could not practise their traditional ways and did not have the skills to live in this new way.

PRACTICE

43. Practice

1 Interpretations A and B both discuss the causes of the Civil War, but offer different views. Interpretation A argues that the cause was a power struggle between slave states and free states over the power of the national government. When Lincoln became president and wanted to ban slavery, seven Southern states formed their own nation. McPherson claims that the Northern states worried the country would collapse into small nations which would fight with each other. Interpretation B, on the other hand, claims that the Civil War occurred because slavery was not compatible with American values of equality and democracy. Du Bois argues that equality and democracy were impossible when a large percentage of the population was not equal, and had no say in how they were ruled.

44. Practice

2 Interpretations A and B might have different interpretations about the causes of the American Civil War because the authors had different life experiences. McPherson is a modern historian writing about the past, whereas Du Bois is writing about something that still affected him personally. As an African American born in the 19th century, Du Bois lived in a society which had directly experienced the effects of slavery. In contrast, McPherson is writing well over a hundred years after the events, so he is not personally affected by what happened. Also, McPherson will have had access to the writing and research of over a hundred years of historians examining the causes of the Civil War, including Du Bois's book. McPherson's interpretation of what he has read and researched himself has led him to focus on the struggle between the federal and state governments as a key cause for the war.

45. Practice

3 Either interpretation could be found more convincing.
- **To support Interpretation A:** I find Interpretation A more convincing because it is written by a historian more than one hundred years after the event, and by someone who will have had access to a lot of different sources of information. It is true that disagreement over slavery, and the power of the national government to stop it, was a major cause of the Civil War. It is also true that the Northern states were worried the country would fall apart if the Southern states were allowed to leave and form their own nation, and that the free states did not want this to happen.
  As an African-American historian and civil rights campaigner at the start of the 20th century, W.E.B. Du Bois had to fight to be treated as an equal and suffered from the racist consequences of slavery. This might have led Du Bois to focus more on the moral and ethical wrongs of the way African Americans were treated, and how that treatment contradicted the values of freedom and equality on which America was founded.

- **To support Interpretation B:** I find Interpretation B more convincing because it was written by someone who had to live with the consequences of slavery and the Civil War. As an African American, W.E.B. Du Bois was well placed to see the conflict between the American values of freedom and equality, and the institution of slavery that kept four million people in servitude. I think that many Americans living in free states before the Civil War would have felt the need to 'appease the moral sense of civilization' that was put in danger by slavery.
  As a historian writing more than a hundred years after the event, McPherson takes a more detached view of the situation which may not reflect how people thought and felt at the time.

47. Practice

4 Any two from the following:
- Most people would use oxen to pull the loaded wagons as they are very strong, but they are also very slow. Timescales for the journey were tight and delays could lead to disaster.
- The routes were dangerous. Migrants often had to face difficult weather conditions such as snow, sandstorms and strong winds.
- The routes were dangerous because of potential attacks by Plains Indians.
- The biggest danger came from illness, and cholera and dysentery in particular killed many. For example, the Sagar Party was hit by typhus, which killed both parents.
- Migrants needed to take enough supplies to last the whole journey, which included passing through two very steep and dangerous mountain ranges, as there was nowhere along the way to buy food or equipment.

48. Practice

5 Answers could include the following:
- The expansion into California increased – as more mining towns grew, demand for farms and lumber-mills also grew rapidly because the towns needed food and wood. California was well suited to farming and very soon began to export produce. In 1850, California became an American state, and San Francisco grew rapidly to become a major city and busy port. The Gold Rush strengthened the appeal of the West and this suggested that 'Manifest Destiny' was coming true. This encouraged the American government to keep expanding into new territory, including Indian lands, leading to more demand for settlers.
- It increased tensions with Plains Indians because more migrants used the Oregon Trail. Many trails crossed Indian sacred sites, such as the Black Hills of Dakota, which made the Plains Indians angry and more likely to attack. This increased tension led to a rise in the number of Californian Indians murdered by migrants.
- The Plains Indians were also angry because mining activity had a negative impact on the land, causing flooding, clogged rivers and the death of wildlife. This made it hard for the Plains Indians to survive and made them even more hostile to white settlers.
- The Gold Rush increased levels of violence because of the mass immigration and widespread lawlessness in mining camps, which led to tensions between different races.

50. Practice

6 Either can be argued to be the more important reason.
For **the Dawes Act**, answers could include:

- The Act split reservations up into smaller allotments, meaning that the Plains Indians no longer had enough room to continue their nomadic way of life.
- Allotments gave 160 acres to each adult and forced the Plains Indians to live on small farms more like the homesteaders did.
- It also meant that they had to live in small families, like most white Americans. Since they no longer lived in big tribes, it broke down tribal loyalties.
- After the Dawes Act, Plains Indians became American citizens just like white Americans. This meant they were required to obey the laws of the American government, which were often not compatible with the traditional Plains Indian way of life.
- Boarding schools were created where children were taken away from their families and encouraged to live like white Americans. They were taught that their own culture was backwards and uncivilised, and punished for speaking their native language or taking part in their native culture.

For **closing the Frontier**, answers could include:

- When the Frontier was declared closed, the land had changed completely. Railroads and settlements were built across the Plains and land was broken up for homesteaders.
- With no frontier to the West, more and more settlers came to land that had previously been thought of as unfit for settlement. Land that had once belonged to the Plains Indians was often opened up to white settlers, such as during the Oklahoma Land Rush.
- After the Battle of the Little Big Horn, the attitudes of white Americans hardened towards the Plains Indians. Many people felt the Plains Indians should either assimilate or die.
- Indian culture and resistance was not wiped out with the Dawes Act – the Ghost Dance movement took hold after the Act was passed, and worried the government because it showed that the Plains Indians were still a threat. This led to the massacre at Wounded Knee.
- Massacres like the one at Wounded Knee were reported as Indian aggression, which led to increased hostility towards Plains Indians, which in turn meant that it was easier to argue in favour of closing the Frontier and placing greater restrictions on Plains Indian culture.

You may choose to argue that both the Dawes Act and the closing of the Frontier were equally significant. You could point out:

- White settlers were afraid of the Plains Indians' way of life and thought they were inferior. After the Dawes Act, the Ghost Dance Spiritual Movement rejected the white American way of life and made white Americans more determined that the Plains Indians should become like them.
- White settlers believed in the concept of 'Manifest Destiny' – that their way of life was superior, and that they had a right to Indian land. They believed that Plains Indians should either be more like them, or be killed.
- Both the Dawes Act and the things that happened during the closing of the Frontier were results of these issues, and led to the decline of Plains Indian culture.

Notes

Notes

Notes

Notes

Notes

Published by Pearson Education Limited, 80 Strand, London, WC2R 0RL.

www.pearsonschoolsandfecolleges.co.uk

Text and illustrations © Pearson Education Ltd 2018
Produced by Just Content Ltd, Braintree, Essex
Typeset by PDQ Digital Media Solutions Ltd, Bungay, Suffolk
Cover illustration by Eoin Coveney

The rights of Sally Clifford and Julia Robertson to be identified as authors of this work have been asserted by them in accordance with the Copyright, Designs and Patents Act 1988.

First published 2018

21 20 19 18
10 9 8 7 6 5 4 3 2 1

British Library Cataloguing in Publication Data
A catalogue record for this book is available from the British Library

ISBN 978 1 292 24285 9

Printed in Slovakia by Neografia

Acknowledgements
Content written by Rob Bircher, Brian Dowse, Victoria Payne and Kirsty Taylor is included.

p 35, 36, 38: Keys, David, Custer's heroic image collapses under investigation: Archaeologists have demolished the myths surrounding a legendary American battle. David Keys reports, in *The Independent*, Aug 14, 1993, © 1993, Independent Digital News & Media Ltd ; **p 42,45**: Dr. McPherson James, A Defining Time in Our Nation's History, https://www.battlefields.org/learn/articles/brief-overview-american-civil-war ©2018, American Battlefield Trust.

Pearson acknowledges use of the following extracts
p 42: Du Bois, William Edward Burghardt, Black Reconstruction, Harcourt, Brace And Company, © 1935, Houghton, Mifflin Company.

The author and publisher would like to thank the following individuals and organisations for permission to reproduce photographs:

(Key: T-top; B-bottom; C-centre; L-left; R-right)
Alamy Stock Photo: Granger Historical Picture Archive 2,20, Pictorial Press Ltd 17, Archive Pics 18cr, **Shutterstock**: Everett Historical 4,18cl,21, Universal History Archive / Universal Images 9, Granger 31, **Library of Congress Prints and Photographs Division:** LC-DIG-ds-04507/Clay, Edward Williams Robinson, Henry R.5,LC-DIG-ppmsca-33072/ O'Sullivan, Timothy H 19.

Note from the publisher

Pearson has robust editorial processes, including answer and fact checks, to ensure the accuracy of the content in this publication, and every effort is made to ensure this publication is free of errors. We are, however, only human, and occasionally errors do occur. Pearson is not liable for any misunderstandings that arise as a result of errors in this publication, but it is our priority to ensure that the content is accurate. If you spot an error, please do contact us at resourcescorrections@pearson.com so we can make sure it is corrected.